WORD ASSOCIATION PUBLISHERS
www.wordassociation.com
1.800.827.7903
TARENTUM, PENNSYLVANIA

All proceeds from the sale of the book will go to Animal Protectors of Allegheny Valley, a no-kill shelter in New Kensington, PA, to help pay medical costs for the dogs and cats housed there.

Copyright © 2022 by Betsy Kay Kennon VMD
All rights reserved. No part of this book may be used or reproduced in any manner whatsoever without written permission of the author.
Printed in the United States of America.

ISBN: 978-1-63385-482-6

Library of Congress: 2022923095

Front cover photo by Andrew Rush

Designed and published by
Word Association Publishers
205 Fifth Avenue
Tarentum, Pennsylvania 15084

www.wordassociation.com
1.800.827.7903

Scooter
THERAPY ~~DOG~~ CAT

Betsy Kay Kennon VMD

Betsy Kay Lemmon MD 2005

*To Karen.
Because without you, Honey,
none of this would have ever happened.*

Prologue

I AM A SMALL-ANIMAL VETERINARIAN. THAT MEANS I TREAT pets, not farm animals. The name is a bit misleading, as some of those pets are bigger than me.

I have wanted to be a vet since I was in the fourth grade. Up until then, I wanted to be my daddy's secretary.

When I was a freshman in college, one of the girls in my dorm got a kitten from somewhere. We were not allowed to have pets of any kind in that dorm, but she managed to keep the cat hidden in her room. After a few days, the kitten got really sick. That girl knew I wanted to be a vet, so she gave that tiny ball of fur to me.

I took it to a local vet, which I really could not afford to do. That man examined the kitten, then told me it had feline distemper (a virus that causes severe vomiting and diarrhea in unvaccinated cats, as well as depleting their bone marrow of infection-fighting white blood cells). He then shook his head to tell me, wordlessly, that its chances were pretty poor.

He gave me advice on how best to treat that poor creature and sent me on my way having charged me nothing. He called it "professional courtesy" for a future colleague.

I followed his instructions to the letter, even skipping classes to care for my little patient. It took about a week, but miracle of miracles, it got better.

I took the kitten, who I had named Shadows, back to see that vet again. The doctor looked at my now healthy cat and smiled. Then he did something I will never forget. He came around to my side of the exam table and shook my hand. I knew then, for sure, I had found my calling.

I entered the profession when women veterinarians were still few and far between. My vet school class at the University of Pennsylvania (class of 1980) was the first class at any vet school in the country to be fifty percent women. Many schools at that time had no female students at all. That's certainly not the case nowadays. Women currently outnumber men in the veterinary field. The reasons are varied. Some are financial, as veterinarians in general earn significantly less than physicians, despite investing the same amount of time and money training for the job. Men, since they often assume the burden of being the primary bread winner for their families, can be discouraged by that. Another reason may be that many people perceive female veterinarians to be kinder and more caring than men. Whatever the case, I am proud to be one of those women veterinarians.

Many people say to me, "Oh, you must love animals!". I do. But to be successful in this profession, you also have to love people. The other end of the leash. I have yet to see a single patient come through my clinic's doors by itself. Nor do any of my patients carry ATM or VISA cards.

I must confess I did have one patient who came into my clinic by himself, and on a regular basis. He was a chocolate lab named Cocoa who lived just a short distance away. His owner's son used to work part time as a helper at the clinic before I started there. Cocoa would show up at quitting time every day to walk home with him. By the time I was working there, that kid had grown up and gone off to college. Yet Cocoa still came to look for him. Once or twice a month he would leave his yard, walk up Fairview Road to Dorseyville Road, turn right, and trot the eighth of a mile to our parking lot. There he would sit at the front door and patiently wait until someone else arrived and opened it. In he came and proceeded to make himself right at home in the waiting room. Which would have been OK with me except that, being a large, drooly, smelly, and not particularly well-mannered dog, he usually wound up terrifying a cat or an owner, or both. To restore our usual peace and quiet I had to take a break between office calls to drive Cocoa back home.

Cocoa was the exception to the rule that dealing with people is a very large part of the job of veterinary medicine. Especially the verbal part. Dogs and cats can't talk (thank God), but their owners sure can. If you don't like dealing with people, you are not going to like being a vet.

I love being a vet. There is no such thing as a dull day in this profession. Ask anyone in it, no matter how long they've been in it, and they will tell you that you can never say you've seen it all. Every day brings something different and new. That is a large part of the appeal of being a vet. I often feel sorry for physicians. In the veterinary world we like to say, " Real doctors treat more than one species." Physicians treat only one species, and most of them treat only one little part of that one species. How boring is that?

I derive immense satisfaction and fulfillment from being a vet, not to mention amusement and joy. Animals are amazing, and animal people are a fascinating and wonderful bunch. Dealing with animals has taught me how to read their body language and respond appropriately, how to trust all my senses, not just the vision humans mostly rely on, and how to listen to my intuition, "my gut", above all else.

Dealing with people has given me insights into the human psyche that could rival those earned with a Doctor of Psychology degree.

I've been in practice for over thirty years, treating dogs and cats and birds and reptiles and rabbits and lots of other critters. I have trimmed the teeth of nasty hamsters. I have taken blood from turtles. I have helped egg-bound birds deliver their eggs. I have done surgery on rabbits. I have given enemas to snakes. (Of all the things I have done in all my years in practice, that is the thing my mother found most fascinating. Go figure.)

I have even vaccinated a cougar. A pet cougar. It was in California; of course it was. The cougar belonged to a young man with waist-long blond hair who arrived dressed all in black leather including knee-high boots. He brought the cat in on a leash, and it walked by his side as calmly as any Labrador retriever. But this was no dog, this was a full-grown mountain lion! The man warned me that, despite her serene demeanor, this cat did not like needles. To give her the shots, we passed her leash under the exam room door, closed the door, and had the owner gently pull on the leash from outside the exam room until the big cat's head was pinned against the floor at the base of the door. That's when she began to yowl like some creature loosed from hell. You cannot imagine how loud her screams were, especially being contained in a small room. I took a deep breath, came in behind her and did my job. Fastest two shots I ever gave. But the very second the shots were over and the owner released his grip on the leash, that gorgeous beast stopped all her noise and was as peaceful as she had been before. My ears, however, are still ringing.

For twenty-three years of my career, I worked at Harts Run Animal Clinic in a wealthy suburb of Pittsburgh, Pennsylvania, my hometown. That is where I was at the time of this story, and I was then very unhappy with my job. I loved the work, but my boss was a jerk. Why do I say that? Let me explain.

I am passionate about what I do. I go the extra mile. I take ownership of every case and follow it through to the end. I treat every patient the way I would treat my own pets and every client the way I would want to be treated. I strongly believe that you have to do all that when you are caring for living, feeling creatures. My boss, not so much. He was the kind of person who just floated along in life, expending as little effort as possible, doing just enough to get by. That's fine for some things. But not for the practice of medicine. We butted heads all the time because of that difference in our approach to practice, which left me feeling frustrated and miserable.

 So at age fifty-four I found myself spending a lot of time thinking ahead to retirement. But when I was retired, what would I do with my time and energies, I wondered? One day it came to me.

Pet therapy.

With my veterinary skills and people skills I could train a therapy dog, and together we could visit people to help them be happier and feel better. That's the ticket, I thought! In ten or fifteen years, when I retire, I would like to do something with pet therapy.

Well, as you know, God hears all our thoughts. But, as I soon learned, his hearing is maybe not as good as it used to be. After all, he is pretty old.

He heard the... "I want to do something with pet therapy," part. But he completely missed the... "In ten or fifteen years when I retire," part.

Next thing I knew, I had a therapy pet.

But it wasn't a dog. It was a cat.

How It Began

"Dr. Kennon! We have a walk-in emergency!" Barb's voice rang up the stairs. I had just settled on the couch in our employee lounge for a short after-lunch snooze. The morning had been a long one at Harts Run, starting with an altercation with my boss, something that had been happening more and more over the past few months. Grumbling to myself, I got back up and went downstairs to the main part of the clinic.

Greg Larson (not his real name) stood in the exam room, visibly upset. He paced back and forth, from the door to the table and back again. Usually he came in with his husky Yukon (not his real name either). Today there was a cardboard box on the exam table, and no dog in the room.

Inside the box was a black and white cat lying very still, its eyes closed. The only movement was its breathing.

"I looked out my kitchen window, and I see Yukon come walking into the yard with this poor cat hanging out of his mouth," Greg cried, shaken. "I can't believe he would do something like hurt a little cat! You know how much I love animals, Doc! I am sick over this!"

A quick exam showed that the cat was in shock and, more concerning, had no feeling or movement in its rear legs. Not a good sign. And it had no collar or ID tag or microchip to tell us who it belonged to.

"Greg," I said as calmly as I could, in an effort to soothe him, "I think this cat is paralyzed in the rear end. You're being a good Samaritan here, bringing it in when it's not your cat. I'm not going to charge you for the exam, but if we want to know for sure what's wrong, we probably should do radiographs of its spine. Do you want to pay for x-rays?"

Generous as always, he said he did. The x-rays showed no fractures or luxations of the bones of its spine, which would have meant the paralysis was irreversible. (A luxation is when two bones are displaced from their normal side by side position. When vertebrae in the spine luxate, that causes the spinal cord to be severed.) Then I took the time to do a more thorough exam.

The cat was a boy. Judging by his teeth, he was about six months old. That is the age when those male hormones kick in and boy cats start looking for a girlfriend if they've not been neutered yet, as he had not been. Looking for love is probably what got him into trouble. Doesn't it always?

Besides the neurological deficits, being in shock, and having a slight pneumothorax (air in the chest, not in the lungs but outside the lungs, where it should not be. It is a common finding after blunt trauma, such as being hit by a car), there was nothing else remarkable about his physical exam.

"Greg," I said, "your dog did not do this. If Yukon had caused these injuries, I'd be seeing bite marks. Yukon was actually the ambulance that saved this cat's life."

Greg exhaled forcefully, obviously relieved. He paid his bill and went home, leaving me to decide what to do now with this cat.

He was a young cat. No owner. And a good chance he'd never be able to walk again. It's hard enough to find a home for a healthy stray animal, let alone one that was going to be permanently and seriously handicapped. The logical course of action was to put him to sleep.

Instead, I decided to wait. I told Barb and the rest of my staff, "Since there's nothing obvious on the radiographs, let's give him the benefit of the doubt. We'll keep him here for a few days and see if he regains any function in those rear legs."

That's what I said to them. What I didn't tell them, for fear they might get on the phone to the funny farm if I did, was that as I was deciding what to do, I heard a voice in my head. It was not my voice. It was not my thoughts. But I heard it as clearly as I have heard anything in my life. The voice commanded me, "Do NOT put that cat to sleep."

I listened and did not.

Several days later, the cat's back half was still useless. His front half, however, had turned into a handsome, friendly, altogether charming cat. He clearly wanted out of his cage to be with people. At lunchtime each day we would lift him out and down to the floor, and off he would go. He got around by sitting up on his rear end, using his front legs to pull his back half along, back legs out to the side. He would scoot that way from room to room and down the halls. That's how he got his name.

Scooter.

And man, could he scoot! He was so fast, we almost had to run to keep up with him. One day Ruth, one of the clinic's technicians, took a shallow plastic Tupperware container, put wheels from a kid's toy on the bottom of it, and laid Scooter's rear end in it. The container was transformed into a makeshift wheelchair for a cat. Once he got the hang of using those wheels to get around, we really couldn't keep up with him!

During lunchtimes we'd let Scooter have the run of the place in his Tupperware wheelchair. The rule was that he had to be back in his cage before appointments started after lunch. But often, we just forgot. On those afternoons I remember hearing many a client, as they waited for me in the exam room exclaim, "Oh, hello! Who are you?" as Scooter would wheel himself into the room and right up to them. He had no fear of people. Rather, he was curious about each person he met. And everyone loved him.

Soon Scooter was spending his days on his new "wheels" in the reception area of our clinic, where the clients could see him as they checked in. We put a collection box on the counter, asking for donations to get him a proper wheelcart, and in less than two weeks had collected well more than the three hundred dollars we needed. We called the wheelcart company, K-9 Karts, to get the process started. They sent us three long pages of instructions on how to measure him. The clinic's technicians did that (not me – I'm hopeless at that sort of thing), and his cart was ordered.

While waiting for Scooter's cart to arrive, I had a revelation. Or maybe that voice I had heard gave me another, quieter, talking-to. This cat really likes people. He is not one bit handicapped by his disability. This cat, I decided, would make a good therapy pet.

Not far from our clinic was a human rehabilitation hospital where people went to heal from injuries and surgery and strokes. I had been there a couple of times, dropping off blood samples for tests that our veterinary lab couldn't run but their lab could. I called their main number and asked to speak to whomever was in charge of their therapy pet program.

Karen Hinkes served as their recreational therapist at that time. I introduced myself over the phone, told her I was a veterinarian, and started to tell her about the cat. We have become good friends over the years, but on that day, I was just some random stranger. As she now tells the story, she was rolling her eyes on her end of the line, saying to herself, "Cats can't do what dogs do! Cats can't be therapy pets!" I was, however, as she likes to say now, "persistent". I don't remember it that way, but after some back and forth, we finally agreed to meet and give this cat a try.

I should have had an inkling, during that first phone conversation with Karen, that my journey with Scooter was going to be unusual in more ways than one. Despite my having told her my name, Karen called me "Honey" as we talked. Karen calls everyone "Honey". But I HATE to be called "Honey." My body tenses up, my jaws clench, and the hair on the back of my neck bristles whenever I hear that word directed at me. Yet for reasons I cannot explain, it did not bother me one little bit when she said it. I still hate to be called "Honey" by anyone else.

Because of that habit of hers, her friends and I routinely call her "Honey." I'm pretty sure my husband doesn't know she has any other name.

His Professional Debut

It was a Wednesday, my day off. I drove to Harmarville Rehabilitation Hospital with Scooter in his sheepskin-lined cat carrier which was seat-belted securely in the passenger seat. He was surprisingly quiet on the ride over, although it wasn't a long drive. Most cats sing loud protest songs when you put them in a car. Scooter did not make a peep.

I parked in the visitors' parking lot and carried Scooter into the big modern lobby. I told the receptionist who we were, asking her to page Karen as I had been instructed. After about ten minutes, enough time for me to start getting a little nervous, she arrived. Karen was an attractive woman, thin, about my age but looked much younger, and vivacious. We introduced ourselves. She bent down to look into Scooter's carrier, oohed and aahed at him, and we headed off into the hospital.

She led us first to a large room where physical therapists were working with about a dozen patients. She asked me to take Scooter out of his carrier. That's when things started to go bad.

Harmarville is a big hospital, with mile-long hallways and enormous treatment rooms. It is also filled with all kinds of large equipment and loud machines, none of which Scooter had ever experienced before at our little veterinary clinic. Food carts taller than me filled with rattling trays rolled by on noisy wheels. Oxygen machines blew loud whooshes of air. Beepers and alarms pierced the air. Announcements blared over the public address system. Instead of his usual curious, friendly self, Scooter was scared. Really scared. When I put him down on the floor, he made a beeline for under the nearest bed. I intercepted him just before he got too far under for me to reach, but we were both rattled now.

Karen, being the nice and patient person that she is, suggested I hold him. With Scooter nestled in my arms we approached a patient who had been watching us with interest, and asked (for the first of thousands of times to come), "Do you like cats?"

The answer was a big, enthusiastic "Yes!" I let out a sigh of relief as Scooter allowed her to pet him.

But the rest of our visit was more of the same. Instead of him scooting around the various therapy rooms we visited, going from patient to patient with his usual engaging charm, he stayed huddled in my arms, allowing himself to be petted and admired but taking any opportunity he could to hide in corners or under beds. I felt so disappointed. I gave up hope of ever being invited back. I could tell Karen was not very happy with how things were going either, although she was kind enough not to say so.

Finally, Karen suggested we try a bedside visit in a patient's room instead of the big multi-person therapy rooms we had been visiting. At this point, we were joined by a floor nurse. We went to room 314, and just outside the door, Karen and the nurse stopped me.

"This woman is a new patient," Karen whispered. "She just came here two days ago. She had a stroke. She is going to be flat."

"Flat?" I asked.

"It means she's not going to talk, she's not going to open her eyes, she's not going to react to you at all. I just wanted you to be prepared."

"But," the nurse said, "her family put lots of pictures of cats on her bulletin board. We think she must like cats."

In we went. There I saw a woman, upper fifties I would guess, lying on her back with her eyes closed, quiet and still, the covers pulled up under her armpits. Across from her bed was the bulletin board, and it was indeed full of cat pictures.

I said, "Hello," in a soft voice, and asked her the usual, "Do you like cats?" I had been told, and have since seen for myself many times, that just because someone seems to be unable to hear you or understand you, doesn't mean they can't. Never assume.

But from this woman there was no response. I gently placed Scooter up on the bed next to her. Then watched in amazement as he snuggled right up against her. Then more amazement as she opened her eyes, started to pet him, and started talking to him.

"Wow!" I thought. "That's pretty cool!"

I turned around to look at Karen and the nurse. Both were in tears.

When she had recovered her voice enough to speak, Karen asked, "Can you come back every week?"

And so, with his first little miracle, Scooter's therapy pet career was born.

Two days after our first visit to Harmarville, Scooter's wheelcart arrived. It consisted of two metal rods that ran along either side of his body, attached to two wheels in the back. A soft rubber tube-like strap ran across his chest just behind his front legs and snapped over his back to hold his front end in place. Another strap ran across his belly just in front of his rear legs, supporting the rest of his body. Two stirrups, made from the same soft rubber tubes, held his back feet off the ground so they didn't drag.

I expected a long training process would be needed to get him to accept being strapped into this contraption, and to teach him how to walk with it. Cats, as a rule, don't take well to new things, and they really don't take well to anything being on their persons that they didn't put there. I was wrong. The first time I put him in the cart, he spent about ten minutes looking over his shoulder as he walked, as if to say, "Why is that thing following me?" That was it. No training, no gradual process of getting accustomed. He took to the cart as if it was a completely natural, normal thing.

That wheelcart was a game-changer. When we returned to Harmarville the following Wednesday, I put Scooter in it while we waited in the lobby for Karen. The cart transformed him into a completely different cat. No more fear, no more apprehension. He strode down those hallways with total confidence, looking as if he owned the joint. I had a leash attached to the cart in case he tried to bolt again for the safety of places I couldn't reach. I never had to use it. Scooter knew, once he was strapped in, that he was there to do a job.

Two weeks after that second visit to Harmarville, I left Harts Run Animal Clinic for a job at another veterinary hospital nearby, run by a man I admired greatly. The staff at Harts Run put Scooter in a carrier and shoved him in my arms as I was walking out the door my last day there. They were afraid my boss would have him euthanized if he stayed there without me. For the five months he had lived at the clinic I had been toying with the idea of adopting him but wasn't sure. That day I knew it was clearly the right thing to do. When I arrived home, I expected my husband to be surprised to see me with a cat carrier. He was not. Instead he asked, "What took you so long?"

Scooter and I fell into a routine. Each day started with a diaper change in the morning, which was repeated in the evening. He was not incontinent, but since he couldn't stand on his rear legs to use a litter box, he wore a diaper just in case nature called at an inopportune time. Changing him was not hard. I would remove the old diaper, then sit him on my lap in my shower stall, his private parts aimed away from me. With one arm I would support his body, while with the other hand I would gently push on his abdomen to get him to empty his bladder and bowels. Although he could urinate on his own, and sometimes did so while diapered, he needed a little bit of help to fully empty his bladder. After he finished peeing and pooping, I would baby-wipe him, put on a new diaper that I had cut a small hole in for his tail, and we were done. On the days we visited Harmarville I added a touch of vanilla extract to his diaper, which helped to eliminate any odors. Tricks of the trade.

Other than the diapers, he was a pretty normal housecat.

Not having a litterbox to deal with was a big plus in my book. And most of the time his old diaper was clean, so dirty diapers were not much of an issue. However one day, not long after he came home with me, he was snoozing in my upstairs library in front of the big picture window when the window washer suddenly appeared on the other side of the glass. That day his diaper was far from clean. Scared the you-know-what right out of him!

Just as an aside, I have been brought to tears standing in the aisle of a grocery store on two occasions in my life. The first time was right after my beloved golden retriever, Davis, died. I was always careful about what I fed him because, as a golden, he tended to gain weight easily and would gladly eat just about anything. For treats, I gave him rice cakes. They are crunchy, come in different flavors, and are very low in calories. I thought they tasted like cardboard, but Davis loved them. The first time I went grocery shopping after he died, I said to myself, out of habit, "I should get some rice cakes while I'm here." But as I turned down the snack aisle, I remembered he was gone, and I broke into tears. Standing in the middle of the aisle, all alone, sobbing.

The second time was the day after I brought Scooter home. I went to the grocery store to buy him diapers. Not ever having had kids of my own, I knew nothing about diapers. How hard could it be, right? Wrong! When I got there, I found an entire aisle, both sides, full of diapers! All kinds, and all sizes! Sizes? Who knew diapers came in sizes? And what size diaper does a cat wear?? I looked around, desperately hoping to find someone to help me. No one was there. The tears started to fall. I somehow managed to calm myself enough to notice that each package had the weight of the child it was intended for printed on the label. I knew Scooter weighed ten pounds. I bought a box of Huggies for seven-to-fourteen-pound kids. They fit. I became a Huggies customer for life.

I never expected to be changing diapers into my sixties. At least they weren't my own.

Our weekly routine settled in, too. Every Wednesday morning at ten o'clock sharp I'd put Scooter in his carrier. Actually, I'd just hold him in front of the carrier, and he would leap inside - as well as a cat with only two good legs can leap. He never balked at going in, never resisted, and once inside never made a sound. He was eager to get to work.

With his carrier seat-belted in the passenger seat, I'd drive to Harmarville, and we'd meet Karen at 10:30 in the lobby. After a few months of this routine, she asked me to park in the employee parking lot behind the hospital, instead of the visitors' lot, enter through the back door, walk down a short hallway to her office and meet her there.

In her office, while she finished up what she'd been working on, I'd put Scooter in his wheelcart. Then we'd follow Karen out into the hospital. She chose which therapy rooms and which patients we visited, and she would guide our interactions with the patients by telling them about Scooter and telling me something about them. Karen taught me much about working with human patients. As we would walk - and with those long Harmarville hallways we did a lot of walking - she would give me the benefit of her experience on how to interact with the patients.

Karen instructed me how to speak to someone who could not talk. If someone could talk, but with difficulty, she directed me to break my questions down to one word, yes or no answers. " Keep it simple," she said.

She showed me how to notice and read the secret signals staff would give each other about a patient's state of mind or status. Karen and her team were relentless when it came to infection control, long before Covid. She knew, or would get the secret signal from another staffer, if a patient had MRSA (a bacterial infection that is resistant to most antibiotics and easily spread from person to person by contact) and would not allow that patient to touch the cat until they had used hand sanitizer. Or if a patient had C-diff (an infection of the intestines that is also easily spread and is not killed by alcohol-based hand sanitizers like most other bacteria are), they would have to wash their hands with soap and water, and she'd get them a soapy washcloth and a towel to do so.

Patients recovering from head injuries, she explained to me, often go through a stage of recovery during which they can become very agitated. She guided me to watch their faces as this was how to know if we should or should not approach them that day, and most importantly to rely on the staff who were working with them daily for advice on how to proceed.

She showed me how to work with a patient's disability. For example, if a stroke patient had limited use of their right side, we would put Scooter on that side as an incentive for them to use their weak arm to pet him. Scooter became part of their physical therapy.

Karen taught me to get at eye level with patients. "Don't stand above them and talk down to them," she said. "That just adds to their feelings of helplessness and loss of independence."

Karen loved to tell the story about our visit with a woman who was quadriplegic. This patient couldn't move her arms at all. All she could do was bend her head forward towards Scooter. But as she did, he stretched his head up towards her till they were nose to nose with each other, much to this woman's delight. And to ours.

People with therapy dogs go through extensive training, both for the dogs and for themselves, before they are allowed to visit patients. No such training for therapy cats exists, as far as I know. I had to learn by the seat-of-the-pants method. I had my medical knowledge and my people skills from my years as a vet, which helped. But most of what I needed to know I learned from Karen.

One day early on, we were walking down another of those long hallways. It was one I had not been in before. Down at the far end I could see an open door on the left side, with about a dozen people in wheelchairs "parked" along the wall to either side of it. I asked Karen what was going on in that room. She told me that was where people got fitted for their prosthetics, i.e. their artificial limbs.

As we got closer, I saw a woman sitting in the wheelchair closest to us with her head down, her shoulders slumped. She was very thin, about mid-forties, with dyed black hair, poorly styled, and multiple tattoos. Her right leg from the knee down was gone. A fresh bandage covered the stump of what was left of it. What struck me most about her was the hopeless, dejected look on her face.

Most of the time on these long hall walks I would carry Scooter, just to get from one unit to the next faster, especially on the days he wanted to sniff and inspect every little thing along the way. On that day he was striding right along in his wheelcart, rolling confidently under his own steam. As we approached, I noticed this woman raise her head to stare at Scooter. She continued to stare, hard, as we got closer and then as we passed her. Just as we were about to turn the corner, I heard her quietly say, "Well, if he can do it, so can I."

That was his second little miracle.

If I had any lingering doubts about what we were doing, Scooter and I, or why we were doing it, they evaporated with that woman's words to herself.

To this day, I get choked up every time I tell that story.

Word Gets Around

HARMARVILLE'S PATIENTS, FOR THE MOST PART, STAYED THERE for just a short time. Every week we would meet new people. As a result, lots of people saw or heard about the therapy cat on wheels. I got my first phone call from a nursing home only a few months after we started at Harmarville.

A woman named Linda called me one day, and asked if Scooter and I could visit Riverside Nursing Center where she worked. It was not far from Harmarville and I was feeling flush with our success there so far, so I readily agreed.

Harmarville Rehabilitation Hospital is a really nice facility. It sits on a lovely campus of grassy lawns with lots of flowers and trees. It is modern in design, with plenty of room (all those long hallways!), an abundance of windows and skylights flooding it with natural light, beautiful artwork and inspiring posters on the walls, and a fresh clean smell. It is a really pleasant place.

I have since visited nursing homes that are also very pleasant. Clean, comfortably furnished, more like upscale apartment buildings than medical facilities.

Riverside was none of those things. The first thing to hit me - assault me, really - as I walked through the second set of doors was the smell. The combination of urine, human feces, strong disinfectant and unwashed-body odors stopped me in my tracks. I had entered a hallway lined with residents' rooms, and many of these residents were sitting in wheelchairs along that hallway. Their appearance kept me frozen in place. These were all very old people, dressed in frumpy clothes, many with food stains down the front. Most had messy, greasy hair. Some sat silently staring off into space. Others were muttering unintelligibly to an unseen audience. Not a one seemed to notice me, or the cat, at all.

I thought to myself, "I'm not sure I can do this." Holding my breath, I somehow forced myself to walk down that hallway to Linda's office.

Now you may be saying to yourself, "Hey! You're a veterinarian! You should be used to bad smells!" And you'd be correct. A typical day at work could have me being peed on, pooped on, puked on, drooled on, bled on, and – that very special feature of all carnivores except humans – anal glands expressed on me. Lots of bad smells!

Aren't you glad humans don't have anal glands? Can you imagine being on a crowded bus on a hot day when somebody expressed their anal glands? Hell could be no worse.

But here's the difference. Those are all animal smells. I am fine with animal smells, and anything else gross on an animal. Pus, maggots, nasty wounds, rotten teeth - none of those bother me one bit. Human smells, and gross stuff on humans, however, are NOT in my wheelhouse.

We made it to Linda's office. She and I introduced ourselves, then I bundled Scooter into his wheelcart and we set off. Like Karen did with us at Harmarville, Linda led the way.

Linda knew every patient by name. She'd say hello, introduce me, tell them about the cat, then encourage our conversation. I'd lift Scooter up, stand his front feet on their lap or the arm of their wheelchair, and hold his rear half while they petted him. We went to room after room, at least two and sometimes as many as six people in each room. All the while Linda seemed oblivious to the sights and smells that were offending me. More than once I felt my stomach lurch as the sight of drool or snot or the sickly-sweet smell I came to learn was what an unwashed body produces overwhelmed me. I had to look away, off to the side and at anything else, till the nausea passed.

Yet as we went along, I found myself noticing the gross stuff less and less. Instead I started to see these smelly old bodies as individuals. A large part of that was due to Linda. She greeted each patient like an old friend, and her obvious affection for them went a long way towards humanizing them in my eyes. Linda would tell me a bit of their story, I would talk to them and sometimes they would talk to me, and always they would brighten at the sight and touch of the cat.

I wouldn't wish a life like they were living on my worst enemy. But into those lives I saw a little bit of joy appear, thanks to Scooter. Another little miracle.

The connection animals make with humans is more profound than anything we make person to person. That connection brought a little bit of happiness to everyone we visited that day. Seeing that speck of joy, time and again, I began to overlook all the bad stuff, and focus on the good. We stayed there for almost three hours that day and visited there every month after that for years. I would still wince a bit at the smell and the depressing state of the residents each time I walked into the building. That didn't last long, though, as I was now looking forward to seeing all the familiar faces again.

As time passed and the word continued to spread, we wound up visiting six nursing homes on a regular basis. Mondays and Wednesdays were my days off from work. Every Monday morning, Monday afternoon, and Wednesday afternoon we went to a nursing home. Wednesday mornings were still for Harmarville.

Half of those nursing homes were just as bad as Riverside. The others were much nicer. Scooter's magic was always the same.

I will confess there were a lot of occasions, over the years, when I just really, really did not want to spend my day off visiting a nursing home. The thought of dragging myself out of my nice comfy home to spend two or three hours in a hot (nursing homes are always beastly hot), smelly, depressing place would have me making all kinds of excuses in my head as to why I shouldn't go.

Let me tell you something. If you are ever feeling depressed about how your life is going, or sad about things you want but don't have, or lonely, or any other blue emotion, go spend some time at a nursing home. It will put your life and your problems into very clear perspective. You will come out of there saying to yourself, as I did each and every time, "I don't have a damn thing in this world to complain about. Not one."

I guarantee it.

Heeere's Scooter!

WHERE ARE MY MANNERS? I HAVEN'T PROPERLY INTRODUCED you to the star of our show.

Scooter was a domestic shorthair cat. Or in layman's terms, an alleycat. He was what is commonly called a tuxedo cat, as the pattern of his black and white fur made him look like he was wearing a tuxedo.

His black fur was a deep, glossy black. Most black cats, seen in bright sunlight, are actually dark brown with faint stripes visible in their fur. Not Scooter. His was solid black. His white fur was gleaming white. Such plain colors, black and white, yet so beautiful side by side.

Most black and white cats have green eyes. Scooter's eyes were a warm gold color. The answers to all the questions in the universe could be found staring into those luminous eyes, or so it seemed to me.

The top half of his face was black, and black circled each eye like someone had applied eyeliner with too heavy a hand. The rest of his face was white, punctuated by a pink nose and pink lips and long white whiskers. All four feet were white - the spats that went with his tux.

Scooter weighed ten pounds, the average weight of most cats. He was not skinny or fat, although the way his body was suspended in his wheelcart made his belly hang down like a big beer gut.

His cart had bright red spokes in its black plastic wheels and matching red soft foam tubes ran under his body to hold him in a standing position, back level to the floor. Two little black straps with red foam stirrups kept his rear feet an inch or so above the ground. The side bars of the cart were silver.

Most people were surprised to learn that Scooter could get out of his wheelcart at any time. All he had to do was shrug his shoulders and it came off. He almost never did that. That was how I knew, with certainty, that he was OK with being in it.

When he walked in his wheelcart, his front feet would pad along with a steady pace. His ears were up, his eyes took everything in, and his body language exuded confidence. The cart didn't make any noise, and for that matter neither did he when he was in it. He never purred or meowed when he was working. He also never hissed or used his claws on any patient, no matter what they did. Frankly, there were a few times I would not have blamed him if he had.

Of the hundreds of people we visited, Scooter calmly tolerated all but three. At Harmarville, there were two men whom he absolutely refused to go near. He would plant his feet and come to a dead stop if we went anywhere close to either of them. I had no idea why. They seemed pretty ordinary to me. They didn't look any different, or smell any worse, than any of the other men we visited. Which made me think they were both probably serial killers or ax murderers. Animals can sense these things, you know.

The third person Scooter didn't want to be around was my father-in-law, Chuck. If Chuck came into the room, Scooter would leave. Every time. Chuck was not very cat-savvy, but even he noticed after a while.

"That cat don't like me," he would say.

I tried to smooth things over, reassuring him, "Oh, he just isn't used to you," or, "He's not familiar with your walker, Chuck." Liar, liar. He was around walkers and people he'd never seen before all the time when we were working.

Truth be told, Chuck was right. Scooter just didn't like him. And, truth be told again, neither did I. Did Scooter sense this in me? I'm thinking yes. Because to the best of my knowledge Chuck was not a serial killer or an ax murderer.

Scooter, like all pets, had many ways of letting me know what he was thinking without using words. Birds, by which I mean parrots, do use words. Most people assume they are just "parroting" the words they hear us say, without really knowing what those words mean. I am not so sure about that.

I used to treat an Amazon parrot named Pretty Boy who often swore, "You son of a bitch!" at me, much to the owner's embarassment. He never screamed that at anyone else. Only me.

A client of mine, whose name was Jim, had a parakeet. Whenever the bird saw Jim, it would say, "Psst! Hey! Jimmybird!" over and over, not stopping until Jim would answer him. It ignored anyone else who tried to answer for Jim. When Jim finally replied, that parakeet would then squawk, "Creep!" and proceed to laugh and laugh, rocking back and forth on its perch.

African grey parrots have been scientifically shown to be as intelligent as the average five-year-old child. Much of that research was done on a bird named Alex, whose owner, Irene Pepperberg, was an animal psychologist at Harvard University, among other institutions. The first African grey I ever met belonged to a veterinarian named Tim, a cardiology resident at the University of California at Davis Veterinary Medical Teaching Hospital when I was an intern there. The bird's name was Janis. She lived in Tim's office in the basement of the VMTH. Tim told me she once declared, "Bad guys have green shit." He assured me he never said anything like that to her, or to anyone else for that matter. Was she just putting random words together into a grammatically correct sentence? Or was she right?

Max was another African grey parrot, and a patient of mine. Max came to see me on a regular basis to have his nails trimmed. He always arrived perched on his owner's shoulder. I tried to discourage bird owners from bringing their pets in without a carrier of some sort. I was afraid that something like a barking dog might spook the bird, causing it to fly to the floor where said dog could attack it, or to fly out the door and be lost forever. But Max always stayed put, even when he saw me coming towards him with the towel I wrapped him in for his pedicure.

Max was quite the talker. You never knew what he was going to say. "I ate some chicken soup," he told me one day. Another time he said, "I'm going to have a cigarette." Often, after his nail trim, he would be back on his owner's shoulder lifting up first one foot, then the other, saying, "Ow. It hurts. Ow." Despite the fact that my nail trimming procedure, which I did with a dremel rotating file, was totally painless.

Max's owner, Lynn, told me this story. She said she had a friend named Carol come to visit her. Max took a real shine to this woman, perching right next to her the whole time she was in their home. Lynn described Carol as being quite buxom, and that was the part of her Max seemed to be most taken with.

The next day, Max said to Lynn, in his high-pitched nasally bird voice, "Carol has breasts." Lynn got an exasperated look on her face while telling me this and asked, "Where did he learn the word 'breasts'? I never use that word! Where did he learn that?" She then said her mother was visiting them that day. She asked Max, "Does Grandma have breasts?"

Max was quiet for a minute. Then he replied, "They're broken."

I have to think those birds knew perfectly well what they were saying. Kind of scary, isn't it?

Other than refusing to visit the two ax murderers, Scooter at work was all cool professionalism. At home, that cool professionalism morphed into normal cat behavior. We never used the cart at home. He would scoot along on his butt, cushioned by his diaper so he didn't get a rug burn. The diaper made a swishing sound as he went along, so you always knew where he was just by listening. Which was, I guess, different from the silent movements of other cats.

He was able to go up my carpeted steps by pulling himself with his front legs. Those strong front legs were also very adept at opening anything he could reach - doors, drawers, and closets. He often opened my kitchen cupboards and stuck his head inside to inspect the contents. I would scold him saying, "Scooter, everything in there is exactly the same as the last time you looked." Didn't matter. He had to see for himself.

Watching him come downstairs was amusing. His front legs stepped down in a normal orderly fashion, but the rear half of his body dropped from one step to the next with an audible "thump, thump, thump." That did not deter him, though. He even came down my spiral staircase with no hesitation, open-backed steps and all, which scared me to death the first time I saw him do it. My dogs and the other cats were all too afraid of those steps to go anywhere near them.

The steps to my basement were also wooden and open-backed, so he could go down them, but couldn't get back up by himself. He went down there often despite that, because that is where the mice were. He was a good mouser, a fact that surprised the hell out of me, considering his paralysis. I think the mice were pretty surprised, too.

When my husband and I retired we bought a twenty-four-foot RV so we could travel with our pets instead of leaving them behind. Scooter was a good RV cat. While we were driving, he settled on a cushy cat bed I kept under the kitchenette table. He stayed put and kept quiet. Once we got set up at our campsite, he acted just like he did at home, except for being in close quarters with the four dogs, probably closer than he would have liked. Everyone got along, even Scooter and our giant, not-very-well-mannered rottweiler Bruno. I have pictures of them sitting side by side looking out the front door of the RV together, the lion and the lamb.

What Scooter really liked about the RV was the queen-sized bed at the back of the vehicle, which had large ceiling-to-mattress windows on two sides. Scooter loved to look out those windows at all the little forest creatures running around outside. I almost dreaded the first night we stayed someplace new because he would go from one window to the other, then back to the first one, then back to the other, all night long. All of this over top of me, as I tried to sleep. I got little sleep those nights.

At home I had several nice upholstered chairs in my living room, heirlooms from my parents. Scooter had no trouble pulling himself up onto those chairs, and sometimes I even found him perched - precariously, it looked to me - on top of the back of one of them. His climbing on them produced large swaths of shredded fabric on each chair. All my previous cats were declawed. I couldn't declaw Scooter without handicapping his movement even more. So I had ratty chairs. The price you pay for living with a rock star, I figured.

Scooter liked to snuggle. Whenever I sat down to read or watch TV, he would come right over and cry to be picked up and put on my lap. But at night when I went to bed, he was still busy doing cat things. If I put him on my bed at that time he would jump right off and leave the room. At two or three AM, however, he would come back into my room, reach up and claw the side of my bed and cry until I got out of bed, picked him up, and put him on the bed with me. A full night's sleep became a thing of the past.

Scooter also cried when he wanted to be fed, or get treats, or go out on the deck if it was a nice day, or any number of other demands. Remember when I said he never meowed when he was working? Not so at home.

I brought Scooter home to live with me in August. That December we put up our Christmas tree next to the spiral staircase, the same place we'd been putting it for the previous nineteen years. Nineteen years of owning at least two, and usually more, cats.

One night that December I came home from a very long day at work, and I was exhausted. I walked into the kitchen, put my purse down, and found myself just leaning on the island, too tired to move. As I stood there, staring off into space, a movement by the spiral staircase caught my eye. I looked up just in time to see the Christmas tree crash down onto the floor. All the red glass balls that had belonged to my mother-in-law, that had been on every tree of my husband's since he was a kid, were smashed to pieces. All the presents, which had been carefully wrapped and arranged at the base of the tree, were soaking wet. I couldn't believe my eyes.

When I looked around to see who was responsible, there was no one anywhere near the tree. Except Scooter. My paraplegic cat had pulled a full-sized Christmas tree to the ground, something no previous cat had ever done. Something I never dreamed a paralyzed cat could do. I was speechless.

Every year after that, instead of a full-sized tree on the floor, we put a small two- or three-foot tree on top of our kitchen island. No way he could get to it up there.

When I first brought Scooter home, I had a peach-faced lovebird named Sprout who I dearly loved. Coolest bird in the world. All my previous cats kept clear of Sprout because he would give them a good hard bite with his sharp beak if they got close enough. So Sprout had no fear of cats. I'm sure you can see where this is going. It wasn't long before Sprout, in one of his daily flights across the living room, flew too close to Scooter. Scooter swatted him right out of the air and was carrying him off in his mouth to finish the deed as I came screeching over to Sprout's rescue.

I had a long talk with Scooter after that. He wasn't one bit sorry.

I also had two other cats when Scooter arrived, both elderly females. One of them, Betty Jean, was a tiny little grey tabby. She and Scooter got along fine. But for whatever reason, Scooter took an instant dislike to the other one, a chubby tabby cat named Kizzy. He tried to beat her up every chance he got. It started the very first time he saw her, clear across the kitchen, and never stopped till the day she died. I had no idea why. It got so bad she spent the better part of his first two years in my house hiding down in the basement. It was the only place Kizzy felt somewhat safe. She spent so much time in the dark down there I was afraid she was going to get ricketts. Every day, when I would go down to check on her, I would tell her, "Kizzy! He can't jump! Just stay up on the furniture and you'll be fine!" It took her almost two years to finally figure that out for herself.

The only time there was peace between them was at mealtime. Each cat got a can of Fancy Feast in his or her own bowl, and while they ate all was well. But Scooter ate fast, much faster than Kizzy. As soon as he was finished, he would make a beeline for her and the pummeling would resume. So I made it a habit to quietly put my foot on his tail while he was eating. He couldn't feel his tail, so he didn't notice. When he would then try to run over to Kizzy, he could only manage little jerking motions in her direction. He never seemed to realize what was impeding him. Poor Kizzy got to finish her meal in peace.

Was that cat abuse? Maybe. Not sorry.

Despite being carried in a husky's mouth - or maybe because of it - Scooter never had any fear of dogs. My friend Paula had just gotten a new rottweiler puppy, Sassy, and they came to visit us in late October of Scooter's first year with me. Sassy was about four months old, so she still had a puppy brain, but her body was already pretty darn big. Being almost Halloween, I had my house decorated to the nines, as usual. Halloween has always been my favorite holiday, and even though I have more Halloween stuff than most people would know what to do with, every year I have to get more. New that year was a life-sized werewolf-skin rug in front of the fireplace in my living room. The head would howl and the eyes would light up red anytime someone stepped on it. Scooter, for whatever reason, loved it. The howling did not seem to bother him one bit, and he spent many hours curled up on that thing.

That's where he was when Sassy walked into the room. She had never seen a cat before and went right over to check him out. She got promptly hissed at and swatted, hard.

Stunned, she backed up six feet, hunkered down, and stared at Scooter while she tried to decide what to do. She made a couple more attempts to approach him, with the same results. Finally she grabbed the closest edge of the werewolf-skin rug with her teeth and proceeded to drag it clear across my living room, through the dining room, and out into the entry hall, cat and all. Scooter sat there, unperturbed, right in the middle of his now mobile furry rug and refused to budge. With that, a very confused and whimpering Sassy just gave up.

I have always had large dogs, including while Scooter lived with me. He paid no attention to them, and they pretty much ignored him. One day in August of 2016, just a week before I was to retire from private practice, a little ten-pound (Scooter size) terrier showed up at my door. My three dogs had started barking like crazy just before five o'clock that morning. If you have dogs, you know that they have different barks for different things. There is the deer bark, the mailman bark, the squirrel bark – this was none of those barks. My husband, not wanting his sleep to be disturbed at that early hour, got up and let them out. I would not have done that unless I knew what they were barking at. I asked him, "Did you look outside to see what was there?" His sleepy reply was, "I didn't see anything," and he went back to bed. About twenty minutes later I let my dogs back in. Only instead of three, there were now four dogs. That little brown dog walked right into my house, underneath the three big dogs. As if he had lived there all his life.

He was wearing a collar, one sized for a much bigger dog but cut short to fit him, with no ID tag. He had no microchip. And he showed no sign of wanting to leave. After some debate, I decided to keep him. I named him Augustus Underdog, Auggie for short.

Like most small terriers, Auggie was fearless, and in his mind was every bit as big as the other dogs. He bossed them around, pushing his head in their food bowls while they were eating and lying down in the middle of their dog beds. He would even rip toys out of our giant rottweiler's mouth while growling ferociously at poor dumb Bruno, leaving

Bruno hanging his head and looking sad. Thankfully, the big dogs were tolerant of this impudence.

One day I was sitting on the toilet when Auggie came running over to me, ears down and body hunched over as if he were really scared. He sat himself quickly right between my feet and froze. "What in the world has gotten into you?" I was wondering, when I saw something else coming into the room. It was Scooter, hot on Auggie's trail with one paw raised ready to swat him a good one. Scooter was obviously way scarier than a giant rottweiler.

My friend Tammy worked as a physical therapist at Harmarville. Everyone else who worked there had only good things to say about Scooter. Tammy delighted in telling patients, as they oohed and aahed over Scooter, about all the BAD things he did. She always told them about him catching Sprout, and about him bringing down the Christmas tree. But this was her absolute favorite story to tell.

It was the Monday before Halloween. As I said before, I am a Halloween nut. I have so many decorations that it takes me a full three days to put them all up. In my living room there is a spiral staircase going up to the second floor, and I always have fun decorating it. That year, it was full of Halloween cats-- lifesized black cats with arched backs and bared fangs, fake cat fur standing on end, ears flat back.

I had spent that morning at my mother's house on the other side of town, helping her with some errands and chores. When I got home I went to gather Scooter as we were scheduled to visit a nursing home that afternoon. I couldn't find him.

I looked upstairs. I looked downstairs. I looked in the basement. No Scooter. I looked again on all three floors, even looking in places he couldn't possibly be. Still no Scooter. By now I was starting to panic. Did he somehow get outside that morning? I didn't think he could have. But if he did, alone outdoors with his mobility issues, he would have been a sitting duck for any coyote or hawk or stray dog that came along. My mind was in a frenzy.

Then out of the corner of my eye I noticed something. Something white, on the spiral staircase full of black cats. I looked closer. On the first step was a Halloween cat. On the second step was a Halloween cat. On the third step was a Halloween cat. On the fourth step.... was Scooter. His white diaper was what had caught my eye. I had been calling him frantically for a good half an hour, and normally when I called him, he either came right to me or chirped a little greeting. That time he had stayed perfectly silent and motionless. I realized I had probably looked right at him maybe twenty times in my search but mistook him for a Halloween cat. I guess he didn't want to go to a nursing home that day!

I stomped over to him, saying a few choice words, and the look on his face seemed to reply, "Damn. She found me."

Whether being dragged on a rug by a half-grown rottweiller, or being called and searched for by a frantic mother, if Scooter didn't want to do something, he just didn't do it.

We did go to the nursing home that day, albeit a little late. Whether he wanted to or not.

Hospice

Scooter and I had been visiting our nursing homes for several years when one day we were approached in one of them by a lovely young woman named, aptly enough, Charity. She worked with a hospice and was visiting one of their patients. This hospice, like many others, did not have a building of its own for its patients, rather would see patients in their homes or nursing homes or hospitals, wherever they happened to live.

Charity asked me if Scooter and I would consider volunteering with her hospice. She was excited to meet us, and very enthusiastic. I was reluctant, however. Like most people I had a lot of misconceptions about hospice care and what it involved. But Charity was very hard to say no to. Eventually I agreed.

That turned out to be a very good decision on my part. Under Charity's guidance, that hospice held lots of classes for its volunteers on all aspects of death and dying and caring for the people involved in the dying process. I went to every class I could. I learned that hospice is really a life-affirming endeavor, not morbid at all.

To qualify for hospice care, a patient needs to have a doctor say they likely have only three to six months to live. But accepting hospice care does not mean giving up. It does not mean accepting defeat. It is not a death sentence. In fact, lots of people "graduate" from hospice, meaning that, due to the high-quality physical, emotional, and spiritual care they receive, they actually get better. They achieve a level of health that no longer requires hospice care.

What hospice care does mean is focusing on life. Making a patient's life as comfortable and meaningful as possible within the constraints of their disease.

I learned about art therapy, aromatherapy, and music therapy for patients. Of course I already knew a little something about pet therapy. I learned about therapeutic touch, even as simple as a hand massage, as a way to connect to a patient who can no longer communicate through verbal means. I learned how to meet someone with dementia where they were. If they were back in 1965 in the kitchen of their mom's house in their mind, that's where you went, too.

I learned that people may linger for much longer than expected, despite how ravaged their bodies are, if they have unresolved conflicts in their lives. People seem to have some degree of control over when they actually die and can put it off until they get a chance to clear the air or clear their conscience from whatever it is that still bothers them. Along those lines, I learned five things you should say to a loved one who is actively dying to ease any possible bad feelings between the two of you....

> 1. "Thank you." Thank them for all they have done for you and meant to you.
>
> 2. "I'm sorry." Apologize for anything you may have said or done to hurt them.
>
> 3. "I forgive you." Forgive them for anything they may have said or done that hurt you.
>
> 4. "I love you." Never let that go unsaid.
>
> 5. "Goodbye." Let them know it is okay to go.

I learned that it is common for people who are dying to suddenly perk up, seeming to rally for a while, becoming lucid and interactive, even asking for specific foods to eat, before falling back again.

One of the best things I learned was from Mike Trenga, the spiritual care coordinator for Charity's hospice. I was telling him about visiting a hospice patient in her home. I saw photos of family members on her wall and, to make conversation, I began to ask her about them. When I got to a photo of her husband, she started to cry as she told me about him.

I told Mike I felt absolutely horrible for making this poor woman cry. He told me, "No, don't feel bad. Those were good tears." He went on to explain that tears like that are good for a person's emotional healing and good for the soul, and that I should never feel bad about tears like that. That was a huge revelation to me, and very comforting.

There were so many other topics I learned about, even what to do in an active-shooter situation. That's the world we live in today - having to learn how to keep from getting killed while you are trying to help someone die.

The knowledge I gained from my hospice training was powerful. It helped me deal with all the patients we visited, not just hospice patients, in a more meaningful way. On a personal note, when my own mother was dying my hospice experience enabled me to know what was happening, what I could and needed to do for her, and what to expect. I was able to communicate all of that to my three siblings as we sat around her hospital bed. That was a truly precious gift.

Visiting a hospice patient was much different from visiting a nursing home. Instead of spending a few minutes with a lot of people, we would spend an hour or more with just one person. Scooter liked it. No walking or being carried from room to room to room. He could settle on a lap or, even better, on a bed. Scooter never met a bed he didn't like. All he had to do was just soak up the attention.

I was surprised at how patient he could be, and for how long. One woman we visited was very restless, almost agitated. She couldn't sit still, constantly fidgeting, and attempting to stand up now and then even though she could only raise her behind an inch or two off the chair. Scooter never tried to get down off her lap. I had to catch him from falling a few times as she moved around, but he never tried on his own to leave.

For me, though, visiting a hospice patient was harder. Making conversation with someone you don't know for a few minutes, even for an introvert like myself, isn't too hard. Making conversation for an hour or more is a challenge. With some patients, communicating on any level was not easy. Some were not verbal at all, and many were very hard of hearing, while others could still speak but the connection between their brain and their mouth was tenuous at best.

The more time I spent visiting and interacting with these patients, though, the more deeply connected to them I became, and often to their families as well.

One of my favorite patients was Mary. Mary reminded me of my mother. She was born the same year, 1919, and was just a few months older than Mom. Her youngest daughter, Terri, was the same age as me. Mary had a private room at one of the nicest nursing homes in town, which distressed her to no end because she felt her kids were spending too much money for it. My mom would worry about spending money on herself, too. Mom refused to buy a new mattress even though the one she had looked like a horse trough ran through the middle of it. My sister and her husband stayed in that bed one night while visiting Mom and spent the whole night rolling into each other.

I told my mom, and I repeated it to Mary, that we kids did not want or need her money. We were all grown and on our own and doing fine. That money was hers, and she should spend it however she wished on whatever would bring her comfort or pleasure.

Both Mom and Mary gave me the same, "Yeah, right" look when I gave that little speech.

Mary had lymphoma, a type of cancer. It was mostly in her liver, which was so enlarged with cancer cells it made her look like she was nine months pregnant despite the fact that she was ninety-six years old. Scooter loved to hang out at the foot of Mary's bed, and to be petted by her. Yet he refused to stay on her lap. I have to think he knew that large abdomen was full of something really bad.

Mary didn't mind. She would happily show him off to any of the staff that happened by. "Look," she'd exclaim, "There's my cat! Come see my cat!"

Mary loved to talk. One favorite subject was celebrity graves. She could go on at length about where famous people were buried and what their graves or memorials were like. She also liked to quiz me, over and over, "How do birds learn to feed and care for their babies when no one ever showed them?" That boggled her mind. The staff at her nursing home told me she was a good piano player, although I never heard her play. I did get to hear her tell me all about the dolls she collected, which she had proudly displayed in her room.

Mary and my mom died within a few months of each other, just like they were born.

I miss them both.

Andy Warhol Was Right

Scooter and I made our first visit to Harmarville in August of 2008. Happy with how things were going there, several months later I decided to branch out a bit. I contacted a facility called Child's Way for severely handicapped preschool-aged kids. It was part of a larger institution called The Children's Home, founded in 1893 to promote the health and well-being of infants and children in Pittsburgh. Famous Pittsburgher (and arguably the world's greatest hockey player ever) Mario Lemieux, through his charitable foundation, provided much of the financial support for Child's Way. Their day care center was for children not sick enough to be hospitalized, but with medical issues too severe for a normal day care to handle. When Child's Way heard that Scooter had his own medical issues, they were excited to have their kids meet him.

Lemieux is one of my all-time favorite cat names, by the way. Get it? "Le Mew?"

We started visiting there once a week. In the spring of 2009 their head of PR called me and asked if it would be OK for them to do a story about Scooter. I agreed. I thought he said it was going to be for their in-house newsletter. Obviously, I misunderstood. On our next visit, instead of just the Childs Way reporter waiting to interview me, I walked into a room full of reporters. And photographers. Both Pittsburgh newspapers, *The Pittsburgh Post-Gazette* and *The Pittsburgh Tribune-Review*, had people there, as did two of the three local TV stations. As Scooter and I walked down the hall to the toddler room, we were trailed by a crowd of paparazzi, cameras flashing and microphones jostling to catch my answers to the questions being fired at us. It was surreal. I was biting my cheeks to keep from laughing out loud.

Not long after that crazy day I got a phone call from a man named Gary Sledge with *Reader's Digest* magazine. *Reader's Digest* wanted to do a story about Scooter.

Reader's Digest!

Presumably they had seen one of the articles from the media frenzy at The Children's Home, although Mr. Sledge did not know for sure how the magazine found out about us. He interviewed me over the phone, a very nice man with thoughtful questions. I'm sorry we never met in person. Then he said I would be hearing from a photographer the magazine was sending to Pittsburgh to get photos for the story.

Tamara Reynolds, from Nashville, Tennessee, was in touch not long after that. She and her crew of two assistants flew into town on the agreed-upon day. On their way to meet me they stopped to pick up a stylist they had hired from an elite hair salon in downtown Pittsburgh. All four of these people arrived at my house on a Wednesday morning.

The first thing Tamara did was ask me to go put on my best blouse, something in a warm solid color. I searched my closet and came back downstairs wearing what I thought was a lovely yellow blouse. She then asked if I had an ironing board and iron. Apparently, my best blouse was too wrinkled for *Reader's Digest* standards.

Now, I know you don't know much about me, but let me tell you I am not a girly girl. I don't fuss with my hair, I don't color it, I only get it cut once a year, and I don't wear makeup. I wore some on my wedding day, under threat of bodily harm by my best friend if I didn't. That was the last time. Until that Wednesday.

As one assistant ironed my shirt in my living room, the stylist sat me down in front of a sunny window and started putting makeup on my face. Then she fussed with my hair, combing and fluffing it this way and that. When she was finished, everyone gushed about how nice I looked. To me, all this makeup and hair foofing seemed like a frivolous waste of time. But, smiling and nodding back at all my admirers, I kept that to myself.

Off we went to Platinum Ridge Nursing and Rehabilitation Center. Only instead of just Scooter and me walking the halls from room to room, it was Scooter and me and three photographers, one carrying this huge round reflective device almost as big as he was, another carrying an assortment of large complicated-looking cameras, and Tamara.

Tamara wanted pictures of Scooter with a patient. At the recreational therapist's suggestion, our first stop was Rose's room. Rose was a tiny ninety-year-old Italian lady with short grey hair and pale blue eyes. Scooter and I had visited Rose many times before. I never saw her outside of her room, but she was always nicely dressed and sitting up in her wheelchair when we visited. Rose was very sweet and loved Scooter. She always remarked how clean his ears were! Sweet or no, Rose was not afraid to speak her mind. When we visited her on the day after her nintieth birthday, she was glowering and loudly complained, "I didn't even get a lousy piece of cake!"

Each time we visited Rose, I would stand Scooter's front legs on her lap and she would lean over and kiss him on the top of his head. Karen Hinkes used to laugh at how often little old ladies kissed Scooter's head. Some of them were not very neat about their kisses, leaving the top of his head shiny wet with their saliva. Karen called those ladies "the slobberers". Rose was not a slobberer.

As always, when we arrived (this time entourage in tow), Rose grinned as she leaned over and gave Scooter his customary kiss. Tamara loved that. "Rose!" she said, "Do that again!" Obligingly, Rose leaned over and kissed the top of Scooter's head again. Cameras clicked like crazy.

Again Tamara cried, "Rose! Do that again!" Rose gave her a sidelong look first, but once again leaned over and kissed Scooter. The cameras clicked some more.

"Rose!" Tamara cried yet again, "Do that again!" This time, Rose turned and looked at Tamara straight on, glared at her for a long minute, then said, "You want to kiss him, kiss him yourself!" I was laughing so hard I had to sit down on Rose's bed.

After we saw Rose, we made our usual rounds of all the patients who wanted to see Scooter, which was most of them. Tamara and her crew took hundreds of photos that afternoon. Some of the patients gloried in the extra attention. Some didn't care. More than a few looked confused.

At the end of a long and, as always, hot afternoon, Tamara was finally satisfied that she had all the shots she needed, and we went our separate ways. Did I mention that it was hot inside Platinum Ridge that day? And that there was a lot more commotion and hoopla than on a normal visit there? If you know cats, you know that when they are hot and excited, they shed. A lot. You may not know, however, that the makeup professional photographers use is much thicker and stickier than your normal everyday stuff. By the time I was ready to drive back home, my entire face was plastered with cat hair. I felt like a Yeti.

As soon as I arrived home, I ran to my bathroom and took a wet washcloth to my face. Bad idea. There were now smeary streaks of makeup colors all over my face and all over my washcloth as well. I was really steamed. I called my best friend - yes, the same best friend who made me wear makeup on my wedding day. She was very much a girly girl and wouldn't be caught dead without makeup. When she answered the phone, I didn't say hello. I didn't say who was calling. I just barked, "How do I get this shit off my face?!?"

She started laughing, knowing who I was and what I was talking about the way best friends know each other, and suggested I try cold cream.

"Cold cream!" I snapped. "I don't have any cold cream! Why the hell would I have cold cream?"

The solution turned out to be baby wipes, which I did have for changing Scooter, and olive oil.

After all that - three people flying from Nashville to Pittsburgh, long hot hours at the nursing home lugging around bulky equipment, stopping to get a written release form signed by every patient they photographed, and grown professional adults making fools of themselves by dangling silly objects and making ridiculous noises so Scooter would look into the camera – after all that, guess how many photos from that shoot wound up in the *Reader's Digest* article?

One. A picture of me and Scooter. That was it.

The cover story of the August 2010 issue of *Reader's Digest* was titled, "Amazing Pets." Along with Scooter, it featured an eight-year-old pug who surfed with his owner on Waikiki Beach; a chestnut horse who helped a twelve-year-old girl deal with her epilepsy; a border collie who helped her owner do housework; a rescued bald eagle who helped its caregiver recover from cancer; and a vizsla who alerted its owners when their son was having severe allergy attacks. The magazine held a contest in its next issue for readers to vote for their favorite "Amazing Pet." Despite a vigorous campaign on Scooter's behalf, orchestrated by yours truly, the pug won.

Come on, really? A surfing pug? What's so amazing about that?

No sour grapes here.

In September 2010, I was asked to be a guest on a national radio talk show, "Doctor Radio, the Frank Adams Show," to talk about Scooter. I could do this from my home, they said. All I had to do was answer the phone when they called, and they would hook me into the show. Only one small problem. We were going to be on the air at four o'clock in the morning.

I set my alarm for 3:45 AM, so I would be awake and reasonably alert when they called. The host, the aforementioned Dr. Frank Adams, introduced me to his listening audience, and asked me some questions about Scooter and our pet therapy work, which he mixed in with a lot of jolly host chitchat. Then he opened the phone lines for his listeners to call in with their questions.

No one called.

Dr. Adams covered the awkward silence with some more jolly chitchat, all the while encouraging his audience to call in. I can't say I was too surprised. Who is up at that hour of the night anyway? And if they are, do they really want to talk about a cat?

Finally, someone called in. Dr. Adams was elated and enthusiastically welcomed the caller to the show, asking him to please tell us what he wanted to know about Scooter.

"How does he go to the bathroom?" was all he said. That was the only caller we had for the whole show.

Having been on call for many, many nights during my career, I was more familiar than I would like to be with how weird people can be at that hour. There must be something about being awake when your body and brain know you should be asleep that messes with normal thought processes. I worked at one practice that had me on call every other night (I don't recommend that, nor did I enjoy it). There we had a client named Edna. Edna was quite elderly and was fairly infamous with all the employees of that practice for periodically deciding that she was soon to leave this world. Usually an injury or illness of some kind would precipitate this decision. The sad thing was, she would then bring in whatever pet or pets she had at the time to be euthanized, so she wouldn't have to worry about what would happen to them when she died. Invariably, sometime later, she would decide she was fully recovered and would adopt a new pet.

One night when I was on call, my phone rang at 2 AM. It was Edna. In a frantic voice, she told me her dog Precious had just jumped off the bed. "Is she hurt?" I asked. "Can she walk?"

"Oh, yes," Edna replied. "She's fine."

"Then why are you calling me?" I groused, trying not very successfully to hide my irritation.

"Well, because she never did that before!" she replied. I couldn't make this stuff up if I tried.

In July 2012, on a normal busy day at work, I was paged by Heather, our hospital manager, to her office. When I got there, Heather told me I had a call from the ASPCA. "They probably just want money," I replied, my mind too occupied by patients and appointments to think, were that the case, why would they be calling me at work? What I heard when I returned the call stunned me. Todd Hendrichs, Senior Vice President of Development of the ASPCA, informed me that Scooter had been selected to receive their 2012 Cat of the Year Award, and we were invited to attend the Annual Humane Awards Luncheon in November at the Hotel Pierre in New York City to accept. On their dime.

Holy Cow!

As I learned, the ASPCA honors a Dog of the Year, a Cat of the Year, and a Kid of the Year at this affair, one of their largest fundraising events. They would be paying our travel costs to New York and putting us up in the Empire Hotel on the edge of Central Park the night before. And prior to all of this, they would be sending a film crew to Pittsburgh (here we go again!) to make a video of our pet therapy work to show at the luncheon.

On August 8th of that year Kate Miliken, a video director and producer from Arizona, met us at Harmarville Rehabilitation Hospital and again we were followed by a camera crew as we went about our rounds. They interviewed me, several patients, my by now friend Karen Hinkes, and Bob Totten, a physical therapy technician and probably Scooter's biggest fan ever, to narrate the video they filmed.

In the video Bob said, "My first impression of Scooter just blew me away." He went on to say how the patients, "even the ones who aren't very much there, just melt when they see the cat. They make a connection," he illustrated by pointing with two fingers from his eyes to the camera's eye, "that's not there before, even with people." In the background you can hear a female patient exclaiming, "That cat's wonderful!" The camera zoomed over to show her smiling at Scooter, standing on her lap, as she said how very comforting it was to pet an animal. Scooter, enjoying her petting, looked pretty comforted too.

Another patient, a young clean-cut man in a wheelchair, started off the video by telling how he was in an auto accident with a deer and was told he would never walk again. But, he added, thanks to the rehab he'd received, he was now walking. "Seeing a cat with wheels instead of back legs makes quite an impression," he said. "It's astonishing how he gets around. It made me feel like there is hope for me."

The video continued with Karen explaining the type of patients seen at Harmarville and how they move through the system there, from admission to discharge. "The patient mindset can go from very scared, to more and more positive as they see the results of their rehab." She added, "They always thank us," referring to me and her and Scooter. Then with a cute little grin she said, "They always ask, 'Can we take his picture?' They never want MY picture. They want his." She put her silliness aside to finish, saying, "We all need that moment of unconditional love. That's what they get with Scooter."

The video closed with footage of me putting Scooter into his wheelcart, then him leading me on the other end of the leash to the nearest hallway to start our rounds, seeming quite eager to get going. In the final scene, music from a string quartet crescendoed as the camera showed a closeup of Scooter in his cart. His rear end was still elevated but his front end was down on his elbows and his eyes were closed as he dozed, something he did quite often when we were working. He never looked very comfortable like that to me but, judging by his demeanor, he must have been.

Various emails flew back and forth over the next few months, from Kate as well as Lindsay Sklar, the senior manager of special events for the ASPCA, and Missy Goldberg, in charge of special events and special giving, and Tonya Fleetwood, a member of their public relations team, and me, working out final details.

On November 7th, the day before the awards ceremony, I buckled Scooter in his carrier in the back seat of my car this time, as my husband Steve and I were up front, and off we went, following our printed Google Map instructions to New York City.

At the same time, a nasty Nor'easter was also making its way to the Big Apple. Driving was stressful and at times treacherous, so much so that we forgot all about our passenger in the back seat. I've told you how quiet he always was in the car. Well, that was true for all our usual trips. About three hours into this trip we were startled by a loud clear voice from behind us.

"Hey! Did you forget about me? Hey! I'm still here. Hey!" Of course, to untrained ears, it may have sounded more like, "Meow! Meow!"

Growing up in Pittsburgh, both Steve and I were no strangers to driving in winter weather, so we made it to the Empire Hotel in one piece. We settled in our room, which was small but nice. Not much of a view, though. All we saw out of our window was the brick wall of the next building, maybe three feet away.

I was a little worried about how Scooter would react to being in a strange room, since besides our pet therapy visits and my clinic when he first arrived, he had never been anywhere other than my house. I needn't have been. He was all about that hotel room, claiming one of the queen beds as his own and scooting his little self over every inch of the room, inspecting everything.

Once I was sure he was OK, Steve and I went up to the rooftop lounge for a drink. That was really nice, watching the snow come down on the big city with all its lights as the liquor eased the tension of the drive. The bar bill came to $67.02 for one beer and one martini. Gotta love those New York City prices.

Back in our room, we decided to order room service for dinner, instead of going out into the storm to get to a restaurant. For Scooter, I ordered a shrimp cocktail. Shrimp was his favorite food. I think I could have taught him to crawl through flaming hoops for shrimp.

The next day we arrived as instructed at the Hotel Pierre at 10 AM, to have photos taken and answer press questions (here we go again!) before the luncheon. They had me and Scooter, and the Kid of the Year, ten-year-old Declan Greg, and the Dog of the Year, Fiona, an eleven-year-old poodle mix, pose in front of a whiteboard covered in ASPCA logos. Just like you see celebrities do at red-carpet events. Once again, I was finding it hard not to laugh.

Declan, at the ripe old age of ten, had started a blog to advocate for horses and to end the cruel practice of horse slaughter in America, and had lobbied politicians in D.C. and in his home state of New Hampshire on behalf of horses. He was a great kid, mature beyond his years.

Fiona was found as a stray in South Los Angeles, dirty and matted and blind in both eyes. Her adopters got her good veterinary care, so she now had some sight in one eye, but not much.

As we were posing for all those photographers, one of them asked me to put Scooter down on the floor next to Fiona, so they could get a picture of the two of them together. I had three dogs of my own at home at the time, and Scooter was OK with them. But he was not a big fan of dogs in general. Fiona, not being very visual, turned to Scooter and used her one good sense, her nose, to check him out...starting at his rear end. This is NOT considered polite behavior by cats. I saw Scooter's ears go back and his one front paw come up as he got ready to swat this ignorant creature invading his private parts, and I thought, "Oh my God, he's going to take out her one good eye!" Fast as a blink I pulled him by his leash to a safe distance away.

The headline in the next day's *New York Post*, next to a photo of a peaceful Scooter and Fiona, was, "The Reigning Cat and Dog." It could have been, "Cat of the Year mauls Dog of the Year at ASPCA affair!" Phew!

With Scooter safely back in my arms after that, I was wandering around outside the hotel's ballroom when I was approached by a photographer for that same newspaper. He nicely, even apologetically, asked if he could get a picture of Scooter without me in it. He pointed to a long table nearby and asked me to put him down on top of it. I hesitated, as that table was covered in a pristine white linen tablecloth with a fancy table skirt. I told him they were probably going to be serving food on it later, so maybe having a cat on wheels that had rolled through God knows what on that tablecloth was not a good idea. He insisted.

I took the leash off Scooter's wheelcart and set him down on one end of the table, then stood back out of the photographer's way. With that, Scooter proceeded to strut like a model on the runway down to the far end of the table, where he gracefully turned around and walked back right up to the camera clicking away at our end. He ended his "cat walk" by staring into the camera, his nose right up against the lens. The photographer was so tickled that he lowered his camera, grinning from ear to ear, and laid a big kiss right on Scooter's head.

The awards luncheon was attended by about five hundred people, some of whom paid as much as $1000 a plate to attend. Have I mentioned how elegant the Hotel Pierre was? It reminded me of the Duquesne Club in downtown Pittsburgh. Tasteful high-end décor, plush carpets, fancy chandeliers, and highly-trained wait staff in immaculate uniforms.

When it was our turn to receive our award, they dimmed the lights and showed the video Kate and her team had made at Harmarville. We then walked out on stage, Scooter leading the way in his wheelcart. I thought the applause, and the sheer volume of people, would spook him. They did not. As always, in his cart he was all business, the consummate professional. I lifted him up and stood him on the podium as I gave the little speech I had spent hours writing and memorizing and rehearsing in my head. I wish I could tell you what I said. I was so damn nervous I don't remember a word of it.

The award was a tall silver statue with a horse on top. The Cat, the Dog, and the Kid of the Year all got awards with a horse on top. No one knew why. After receiving our award, we were seated back at our table. Lunch was mustard-crusted Scottish salmon with asparagus and chocolate mousse for dessert. Waiters filled and refilled wine glasses generously. I tried to share my salmon with Scooter, but he wouldn't eat a bite. Often after our mornings at Harmarville, I would stop and get sushi for him and me for lunch, our little treat. I got to eat the rice. He got to eat the fish. But only tuna. He was never much for salmon, even as gourmet as this. If they had served shrimp, that would have been a different story.

After lunch, I stood outside of the ballroom with Scooter in my arms, greeting guests and accepting thanks and congratulations from many. One woman, very wealthy judging by her clothes and jewelry, came up to us, tottering a bit on her expensive high heels (as I said, the wine flowed freely at lunch). She never looked at me, nor said a word to me. She just fixed her eyes on Scooter, smiling broadly. When she got right in front of us, she leaned over and kissed him, a long noisy smooch, right on the top of his head. Since Scooter was in my arms at the time, I felt like my personal space was being pretty seriously invaded. She then lifted her head and finally addressed me, saying in a thick European accent, "He looks just like George Clooney!" She went on to tell me her cocker spaniel looked just like Marlon Brando, so consider the source.

An OB/GYN client of mine, Dr. Sheila, years before this had just purchased a sharpei puppy, which she was over the moon in love with. For those of you who may not be familiar with that breed, they are known as the wrinkle dogs. Their skin and fur form massive wrinkles all over their bodies and faces, giving truth to the expression "so ugly they're cute." Dr. Sheila wanted to take her new bundle of joy to the hospital where she worked so she could show her off to her coworkers. But, like most hospitals, this one expressly prohibited animals being on the premises. Not to be deterred, Sheila wrapped her puppy up in one of the blankets the hospital used to wrap newborn babies and cradled her in her arms like you would a human baby. With the puppy thusly disguised, she was walking down a corridor carrying her pooch when she passed a couple of interns chatting. She smiled at them and kept on walking. As she got a little further down the hall, she overheard one of them say to the other, "That is the ugliest baby I have ever seen!" They probably would not have seen the resemblance between Scooter and George Clooney either.

When the event wound down, we took a taxi back to our hotel and packed up for the drive home. We were exhausted but elated. Unlike the day before, during the drive back to Pittsburgh we did not hear one single peep from the back seat. Come to think of it, it was pretty quiet up front, too.

Back home, I got in touch with Patty, a receptionist who had worked at Harts Run Animal Clinic when I was there, and still did, and asked her if she would track down the owner of the husky that had carried Scooter home back in 2008. I did not have any contact information for him, but I wanted him to know that his dog had saved the life of the ASPCA Cat of the Year.

In February 2014 I got a call from a man named Zach Sundeluis. He identified himself as the associate producer of a company called Lisa Erspamer Entertainment. They had recently published a book called *A Letter To My Dog*, which was very successful, and were now putting together a second book called (you guessed it) *A Letter To My Cat*. These were letters written by all sorts of people, some celebrities, and some ordinary folks. They wanted this ordinary folk to write a letter to Scooter for them. No guarantee, Zach said, that my letter would be included because the publisher had the final decision on that, but would I be interested in submitting one? Absolutely I was.

Lisa Erspamer and her team spent a year reading letters submitted from all over the country, and some from beyond. Here is my letter.

> "Dear Scooter,
>
> "I've had dogs and cats all my life. And I've been a veterinarian for over thirty years. So I have had many close relationships with animals. But none of them even begins to compare to my relationship with you.
>
> "I'll never forget the day you came into my life. One of my clients rushed in with you in his arms. His dog had just carried you into his yard, and you were obviously badly hurt, and because he assumed his dog was responsible for your injuries, he was very upset.
>
> "My first look at you was pretty bleak. You were in shock, just lying there on my exam table. And you had no feeling or movement in either of your rear legs, so I knew your spinal cord was shot. But there weren't

any marks anywhere on your body. I searched. So I was able to reassure the dog's owner that his dog had not caused your injuries. Why that dog carried you home, I still wonder to this day.

"What happened next, I cannot explain. We took an x-ray and saw that one of your vertebrae had been crushed, so there was no real hope you would ever regain the use of your rear legs. You were only about six months old, I could tell by your teeth. And you had no collar or microchip, no way for us to contact whoever might have owned you. The logical thing to do was to put you to sleep. But as I was thinking this – and feel free to get a shrink on speed dial when I say this – I actually heard a voice in my head say, "Do not put this cat to sleep." So I didn't.

"Over the next few days, you managed to charm the pants off everyone at the clinic. One of the techs made you a Tupperware box with a wheel on the bottom, and we would put your limp rear end in it and delight in the way you scooted yourself all over the place – hence your name.

"So it dawned on me – you liked people and you were not one bit distressed by your disability. And that, my dear cat, was the beginning of our partnership. You see, you are not just a pet to me.

"You and I are working partners, a team, like policemen and their police dogs. For more than five years now we have visited our local hospital and three nursing homes once or twice a week.

"I remember when you performed your very first miracle. We came to the room of a new patient. The therapist and the nurse who were with us took me aside before we went in and told me this woman would be "flat." When I asked what that meant, they said she had just had a stroke and would not speak or open her eyes. But they thought she might like cats, as her family had put some photos of cats on her bulletin board.

"I lifted you, cart and all, up onto her bed and gently placed her hand on your head so she could feel you. You, my magic cat, somehow knew to snuggle right up against her. And don't you know, she opened up her eyes, smiled a great big smile, and started talking a blue streak to you while she petted and petted your head. I thought, Wow, that's pretty cool! But I didn't realize just how cool until I turned to look at the therapist and the nurse. They were both in tears.

"Since then, there have been more miracles than I can count. Your disposition is so sweet and calm, your fur is so soft, and you are such a handsome cat that you are just perfect for the job we do together. Having a permanent disability that you can show the world is not a handicap to you – it's just icing on the cake.

"There were so many coincidences that brought us together and started us on this path that I have to believe the big guy upstairs had a hand in this.

"Whatever the case, I am eternally grateful to Him, and to you, for all you bring to my life and to the lives of others.

"I love you. I just hope you know how much.

"Love, Mom"

Sixty-four letters made the book when it was published in the fall of 2014. The authors included Mike Bridavsky, the owner of a very famous cat called Lil Bub, and Anne Burrell, a Food Network star chef. Jackson Galaxy, star of Animal Planet's "My Cat From Hell" made the cut, as did Mariel Hemmingway, and Kathy Ireland of *Sports Illustrated* Swimsuit Issue cover-girl fame, and Joe Perry of Aerosmith, and comedian Fred Willard, and TV's physician to the world Dr. Mehmet Oz.

And me.

That December the Associated Press did an article entitled "Purrfect holiday gifts for feline fans," about four giftworthy books for the cat lovers on your holiday list. *A Letter To My Cat* was one of them. And while several of the famous authors were mentioned by name, only one author was quoted for the story.

Again, me.

(Sharp-eyed readers will notice some discrepancies in this story from what I have previously written. My letter was edited by the publisher before the book came out.)

The Pittsburgh Post-Gazette and *The Pittsburgh Tribune-Review* both did stories about Scooter and his upcoming ASPCA award in October 2012, a week or two before our trip to New York. *Woman's World Magazine* had done a story on him the previous April, a full page in their "Inspiring Animal" section. And *Cat Fancy Magazine* did a two-page spread on him in their April 2013 issue. It was in their "Lifestyle, Cool Cats" section, and was titled, "Scoot Over, Disability."

Over the years we were also featured in the newsletters of some of the nursing homes and hospices we visited, such as Golden Living's "Inner Circle," Oakmont Center's "The Oakleaf," Heritage Hospice's "Hospice Volunteerism," and Platinum Ridge's monthly publication. Harmarville Rehabilitation Hospital featured him in "Harmarville Headlines" and again, years later, on the cover of the "Healthsouth Harmarville Newsletter." He was also the photo for April on their 2019 desk calendar, the only month to feature a cat. There were three months that featured dogs.

Even VCA Animal Hospitals, the corporation that bought the hospital where I worked, did a story about Scooter in their *"Woof Wired"* publication and put him at the top of their Facebook page. My hospital manager told me a few days later that he had received 15,421 likes on Facebook. I don't have a Facebook page, so I asked, "Is that good?"

"Yes!!!" she exclaimed.

The Pittsburgh Tribune-Review did another story about Scooter in 2017, interviewing and photographing us at Platinum Ridge, the same nursing home as the *Reader's Digest* photo shoot. *The Pittsburgh Post-Gazette* did a second story on him in March of 2016. The reporter for both of the PG's stories was a woman named Linda Wilson Fuoco. We had not met in person when she wrote her first story back in 2012. She interviewed me over the phone and sent a photographer to Harmarville to get pictures for her article. But she did spend a morning with us at Harmarville for her second story and became completely smitten with Scooter. So much so that years later when she wrote a story about an animal shelter I volunteered for, she included two full paragraphs about Scooter in that article even though he had nothing to do with the shelter. She would go on to write about him one more time, but I'll get to that later. Much later.

We even made it on TV. Dave Crawley, a long-time reporter for local Pittsburgh TV station KDKA-TV, was known for his human interest stories that always ended with an amusing little poem. He spent a morning with us at Harmarville. When he phoned me to arrange a meeting, his very first words to me were, "Thank you for what you are doing with your cat." I was quite touched. Dave was not a handsome man but had a lovely deep voice and a huge heart. I can attest, having seen it firsthand, that his poems were not pre-written or rehearsed. At the end of our filming, he seated himself on the bare floor of a hallway to get close to Scooter on his level, and he popped out a poem about him right off the top of his head.

I think Andy Warhol underestimated Scooter's minutes of fame. Not that I blame him. How could anyone have predicted that a little black and white stray cat would become such a media darling?

Stories

"If you ever wonder why you ride the carousel,
You do it for the stories you can tell."

- Jimmy Buffett

Every visit to a nursing home or to a hospice patient or to Harmarville Rehabilitation Hospital resulted in stories. I'm sure I've forgotten many of them. But here are some that are unforgettable.

Irwin

Our visits to Harmarville usually ended in the occupational therapy room. With several patients in their wheelchairs pulled up to a big table, Karen Hinkes would put a sheet on top of the table and I'd put Scooter, in his cart, up on that. Most patients loved seeing him, and happily petted him and gave him treats. Not Irwin.

Irwin was a sour-looking man in his late seventies who sat silently staring at Scooter, and at everyone else for that matter. In the four weeks of his stay he had spoken only one word. "No!" Whatever you asked him, his answer was a grumpy and emphatic, "No!"

"Irwin, do you like cats?"

"No!"

On this day when our visiting time was just about over, I stood up and walked around the table to pick up Scooter. Just before I reached him, Scooter did something he had never done before and never did again. He fell off the table. Right into Irwin's lap.

All hell broke loose. I scrambled to retrieve my cat, who by now was halfway out of his cart, while nurses and therapists fluttered and fussed over Irwin, asking him over and over, "Irwin, are you OK? Irwin, Irwin, are you OK?"

To the complete surprise of all of us, Irwin replied in a loud, perfectly clear voice, "Well, I guess I'll be alright." The first and only thing other than "No!" he'd said in four weeks. For the rest of his stay, I'm told, he continued to talk.

The cat-drop technique of speech therapy. Who knew?

Ipad

In that same occupational therapy room one day was a young man with an ipad on the table. These things were relatively new at the time and I had never seen one. When Scooter walked over to the man, the movements on the screen caught Scooter's attention. The man said there was an app on the tablet designed just for cats, and he proceeded to bring it up. The app displayed a fish swimming around on the screen. Scooter stood over it, fascinated. When he reached out a paw to touch the fish, it disappeared in a cloud of bubbles, only to be replaced by two fish. My cat was completely entranced.

"You need to get him an ipad," the young man said.

"I am not buying my cat an ipad," I replied.

"Christmas is coming," he said, with a grin.

"Then he better write a letter to Santa Claus," I groused, "because I am not buying my cat a damn ipad!"

You can call me Ebenezer. I've been called worse.

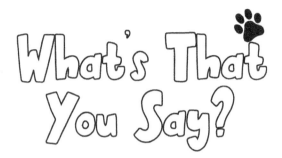

What's That You Say?

MANY OF THE PEOPLE WE VISITED WERE HARD OF HEARING, and my soft voice didn't help matters any. When what I said and what they heard were two different things, it made for some amusing conversations. For example, one time I asked a lady, "Would you like to see the kitty?" and she replied, "I didn't take any vitamin C!"

Yet one conversation happened so many times, with so many different people, it got to be a joke between Karen Hinkes and me. A patient would ask, "What's his name?"

"Scooter," I'd reply.

"Tooter?"

"No, Scooter."

"Tooter?"

"Scooter!!!"

"Tooter," they would say, with a satisfied and approving nod.

Close enough.

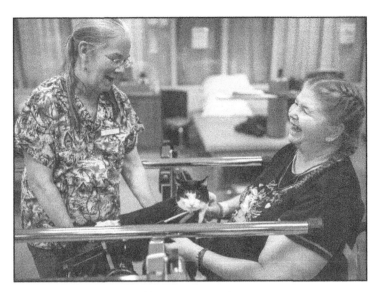

Scooter at work.

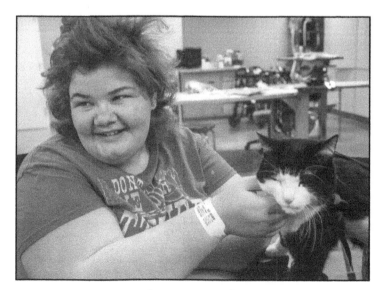

Scooter at work.

Scooter meeting the chickens for the first time.

Scooter snuggling with Betty Jean, the cat he liked, while poor Kizzy kept as far away as possible.

Scooter enjoying a shrimp.

Scooter on <u>his</u> bed at the Empire Hotel in New York City.

The Dog of the Year, Fiona, & The Cat of the Year, Scooter.

Paparazzi at the ASPCA awards ceremony.

Scooter and the giant rottweiler Bruno, in the RV.

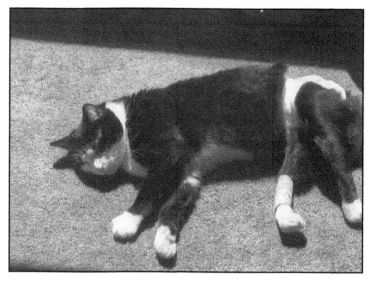
Scooter basking in the sun in my library.

Lossie

LOSSIE WAS A WOMAN WITH SKIN THE COLOR OF MOCHA and very little hair on her head, when she wasn't wearing her wig. She had a ready one-eyed smile (her left eye never quite opened), and a soft clear voice with a slight Southern drawl. When we first met Lossie, she was 101 years old. On her nightstand she had a framed letter from President Barack Obama congratulating her on the accomplishment of living for one hundred years.

I saw Lossie up in her wheelchair only twice. Most of the time she was tucked in her bed, propped up on pillows, either dozing or munching on the last of her lunch. Yet for all of her years she was not the least bit hard of hearing and still mentally sharp and clear.

One September day we entered Lossie's room, and as I greeted her, I said, "Lossie! Today is Scooter's birthday!" I don't know what day in September Scooter was born. I just know he was six months old in March, when I got him. Every time we visited a place in September, I told all the people there that it was his birthday. We only visited the nursing homes once a month, so I got away with it there. But at Harmarville, on the second or third weekly visit in September, someone usually looked at me suspiciously and said, "Hey! Wasn't it his birthday last week?"

Lossie smiled her one-eyed smile and cooed and fussed over Scooter for a few minutes. Then she looked up at me and asked, "How old is he today?" Lossie, at that time, was 102.

I answered, "He's two years old today."

"Oh, chile!" she grinned. "You're gettin' old!"

Cracked me up.

Lossie, part two

I THINK WE SAID GOOD-BYE TO LOSSIE ON A WEDNESDAY IN 2013. She was then 105 years old.

She had seemed really tired for the previous few months. Once she was sleeping so soundly, I couldn't wake her up, although I didn't try all that hard. When she wasn't asleep, she still greeted us with a smile and a warm hello. But that was about it. I kept our visits short, and always told her how glad I was to see her and that she was one of Scooter's favorite people.

That Wednesday when we first passed by her room, she appeared to be sound asleep again. We went across the hall to the recreation room where people were playing bingo and visited there for a while. On the way back I stepped into Lossie's room and up close to her bed and softly called her name. Her right eye opened right up, and she smiled as big as ever. She then surprised me by reaching her right hand out from under her covers to scratch Scooter on the underside of his neck. She kept scratching and scratching, all the while sweet-talking him and smiling.

Lossie had never touched Scooter before. Never. She always welcomed him onto her bed, and talked to him and to me, but she had never once in four years touched him.

After a while, her scratches started getting slower. I said to her, "Lossie, you look tired, so we won't stay. I'm really glad we got to see you today."

She looked straight at me, a serious expression on her face, and said, "I hope I get to see you again." Something about her felt so different.

We never did see her again.

Bless His Heart

ONE OF THE NICEST THINGS ABOUT VISITING PATIENTS with a pet was how many times I got thanked, and in how many different ways. I am not particularly religious, but I heard "God bless you" a lot and was always happy when I did. I don't think you can ever get too many God-blesses. But I especially liked it when someone would say to Scooter, "Bless his heart!" as lots of people did. That expression sounded so charming to me.

Several years ago my husband Steve and I went to Savannah, Georgia, to visit an old high school buddy of mine. Mike was born and raised in Pittsburgh, but he moved to the South when he married a Southern belle, Patty, and had lived there ever since.

Over drinks (one does most everything in the South over drinks) I was telling them how much I loved to hear people say to Scooter, "Bless his heart." Mike and Patty exchanged a funny look with each other, then Patty said to me, "Well, that's not really a nice thing to say." She went on to explain that in the South, if you say something unkind about someone, you typically follow your nasty remark with, "Bless his heart." In reality, it was a snarky thing to say.

Later on during dinner, I was telling them about meeting the latest girlfriend of another of our old high school crowd. I told them that she was fat. Patty said, "Well, now, I could stand to lose some weight."

I replied, "Patty, we could all stand to lose some weight. That's not what I'm talking about. This woman is fat!"

There was a short pause. Then, in perfect unison, Mike and Patty said, "Bless her heart."

Touché. I'm pretty sure, however, there was no snarkiness intended when people said that to Scooter.

9
Don't Let The Wheelchair Fool You

Any time Scooter and I met someone for the first time, I was always cautious in my approach. Some people got spooked by seeing a cat, especially in a place they never expected to see one.

Beulah was a tiny elderly African American woman sitting quietly in a wheelchair in the physical therapy room at Harmarville when I first saw her. When I asked her, carefully, if she liked cats, she immediately brightened and enthusiastically assured me that she did. Then she saw Scooter, and his wheelcart, and pronounced, "Don't let the wheelchair fool you."

I wholeheartedly agreed. I had said to many people, many times, that Scooter's disability was no handicap for him. I have seen many animals during my career with all kinds of disabilities, who carry on their lives as if nothing was wrong. The secret, in my opinion, is that they don't dwell on what could be, as we humans are wont to do. They play the hand they are dealt.

One of my own cats, Zaney, was born blind. You would never know it, though. I am severely embarrassed to admit that he was almost two years old before I realized he couldn't see. What kind of a vet doesn't know her own cat is blind? In my defense, his eyes looked perfectly normal, and they even worked normally. His pupils would dilate in dim light, and constrict in bright light, just like any visual cat's would. The problem was with the connection from his eyes to his brain, not the eyes themselves. In addition to appearing normal, he learned how to navigate his world by following his sister Betty Jean, who I adopted at the same time as I adopted him. He did everything she did.

I found him one day sitting on top of the picnic table in my yard. How does a blind cat even know a table is there, let alone where and how high to jump to get up on it? That amazed me. His disability was not much of a handicap for him, either. Well, maybe just one time.

Zaney had a favorite toy. It looked like a duck in a Santa Claus suit. We called it Santa Duck. Any time he came across it, he would pick it up in his mouth and carry it around, all the while yowling loudly. "I found Santa Duck, I found Santa Duck!" After being awakened in the middle of the night by the Santa Duck yowl a few times, my husband and I made a point of finding that toy and putting it out of Zaney's reach before going to bed each night.

One night I was startled awake at four AM by the Santa Duck yowl. It was coming from somewhere downstairs. I groaned, "Did we forget to put that damn thing away last night?" My alarm was set for five AM, so I squeezed my eyes tight shut and stayed put in bed, trying to salvage as much of my final hour of sleep as I could. Soon I heard Zaney, still yowling, coming up the stairs. He came into my room and stood next to my bed, yowling the whole time. Finally, after what seemed like forever, he shut up and left.

This was early springtime. As a gardener, I had a plant stand out on our porch full of little seedlings that I had started. As they did most years, the mice had been invading my baby plants at night, eating them and the seeds they were growing from. To protect my green babies, I had put mouse traps all around them. That night, one unfortunate mouse had been caught in a trap, not by the neck as they usually were, but around its middle. In its death throes, it had managed to fall, trap and all, onto the ground. Which is where Zaney found it. The one and only mouse he had ever caught in his whole life. He didn't know it was already dead, and he couldn't see that it was attached to a trap. All he knew was that he had caught a mouse, and he wanted his mom to know. Which is why he carried it all the way upstairs to my bedside, yowling with pride the whole way.

When my alarm went off and I turned on the light, I saw what Zaney had left next to my bed. I'm not much of a morning person, but I started to laugh like crazy. "Good job, Zaney!" I called to him. "Good job! You caught a mouse!"

I had a client bring me one of his barn cats years ago whose right front leg had been badly injured. I told him the damage was not reparable, and that we needed to amputate the leg. He was deadset against that idea, saying there was no way a three-legged cat could handle life on the farm. I spent a good bit of time and effort trying to convince him otherwise, telling him the three-legged cats I had seen before got along so well you almost forgot they were missing a limb. Finally, he reluctantly agreed to the surgery. The amputation went well, and I sent the cat home the next day. Two days later my receptionist told me that same guy was on the phone for me. I fearfully took the call, fully expecting him to blast me with a bunch of "I told you so's". Instead, he said he was calling to tell me that he had been unable to find the cat that morning. When he went looking for it, he discovered that it had climbed up a ladder into the hayloft of the barn. On three legs. Told you so.

I remember meeting a dog when I was an intern in California. He was a big dog, German shepherd size, thin, with only two legs. He had a right front leg and a left rear leg. When I first saw him, he was walking down a long hallway, and was having no trouble doing so. When he stopped, however, he made sure he was right next to the wall so he could lean against it. He could walk normally on two legs, he just couldn't balance on them well enough to stand.

I asked his owner how he lost those two legs. He told me that he had been shot by a neighboring farmer when the farmer caught him trying to mate with his dog. Twice. He lost one leg the first time he was shot, and the other leg the second time. I then asked him why we were seeing his dog at the veterinary hospital today. He told me that same farmer had caught the dog trying to mate with his female dog, again. And had shot him, again. (Thankfully this time the gunshot wound was only superficial.)

Trying to mate, on only two legs. No handicap with that disability!

After asking me questions about Scooter and all he could and did do, Beulah started to tell me a story about herself.

She said she was at Harmarville recovering after her third stroke. During her recovery from her last stroke, she had been invited to go play bingo with a friend. She was in a wheelchair at that time, too.

Her friend, she said, made a point of warning her about a really mean man that went to this bingo game and told her it was best to just ignore him, or avoid him altogether.

As they entered the bingo hall, she found herself looking right at this man who was glaring back at her. He growled, "What are you looking at?"

"What are YOU looking at, motherfucker?" she replied. "I could take you out right now! Don't let the wheelchair fool you!"

At this point in her story I was laughing so hysterically I had to sit down.

Beulah went on to say that, over time, she and this man actually became friends. One day he said to her, "I never had no woman talk to me the way you did."

And she replied, "Well, I never had no man talk to me the way you did! And I've had three men in my life. Two were mine, and one was married to my best friend. They're all dead now."

She said his eyes got real big as he looked at her and asked, "Did YOU kill them?"

Don't let the wheelchair fool you.

Chewing Gum

SCOOTER HAD THIS WEIRD THING HE DID SOMETIMES WITH his mouth. It looked for all the world like he was chewing gum. I had no idea why he did this. This was embarrassing because, as a veterinarian, his veterinarian, I should have known. I had examined his teeth a hundred times. I'd had them professionally cleaned. I'd had them x-rayed. Everything looked completely normal. I had no clue.

Of course everyone who saw him doing it asked me, "What is he doing with his mouth?" Most of the time I explained to them what I just explained to you. It got pretty tiresome giving the same spiel over and over again. Especially since it irked me so much not knowing why he did it.

He didn't do it every day but some days he did it a lot. This was one of those days. We were coming out of the physical therapy room at Harmarville. There was a man, Mike, in his mid-forties, parked in his wheelchair against the wall of the hallway outside PT. He was eager to see the cat, and as we were visiting with him Scooter started doing that mouth thing. I went through the whole song and dance again and ended by saying, exasperated, "Usually I just tell people he is chewing gum."

A little while later Scooter and I came back down that hallway and found another man, Bob, about the same age as Mike, now parked in a wheelchair next to Mike. Mike waved us over, saying to Bob, "You have to see this cat!" Once again, Scooter started with the mouth thing.

When Bob asked, predictably, "What is he doing?" I just did not feel like going through the whole explanation one more time. I simply answered, with a wink at Mike, "He's chewing gum."

Bob looked quizically at the cat, then at me, and asked, "Where did he get gum?"

"He takes it out of my purse," I said with a straight face.

Bob now looked really puzzled, and was studying my lip-flapping cat when Mike piped up, "Yeah, want to see him blow a bubble?"

At which point Bob shot Mike and me an annoyed glare and said, "You guys are jagging* me, aren't you?"

Guilty as charged, we had a hearty laugh.

*Pittsburghers have their own special language. "Jagging" is Pittsburghese for teasing or fooling or making fun. N'at.

Wilma

Wilma always sat motionless in her wheelchair clutching her baby doll, a life-sized doll with a rubber head and white cloth body. She never seemed to notice us or anything else for that matter. The only thing that ever changed about her was her location. Sometimes her chair was parked in the hall up against the wall. Other times she was parked in front of a TV in the lounge. Occasionally she was parked in her room, beside her bed.

Wilma lived at Riverside Nursing Center where my friend Linda, the recreational director, would escort Scooter and me on our rounds. On previous visits we had never stopped to talk to Wilma. I assumed she was one of those patients who was cognitively too far gone. One day Linda surprised me by calling out to Wilma as we entered the TV lounge, "Wilma, do you like cats? Would you like to see Scooter, our cat?" No response. Blank expression.

Linda took Wilma's wheelchair and turned it around so she was facing us. "I'll take your baby," Linda said gently.

I expected a protest, but Wilma meekly let Linda take the doll out of her arms.

"Hello," I smiled at Wilma, as I placed Scooter on her lap. "This is Scooter."

Slowly her eyes came into focus, first looking straight ahead, then at me, then at the cat. Her right hand was clenched tightly shut.

"Open your hand, Wilma, so you can pet him," Linda coaxed as she patiently, finger by finger, pried her hand open. "I know you can do it."

Surprisingly, each hard-fought open finger stayed open. Linda took her now flat hand and placed it on Scooter's head, and moved it up and down, stroking him with it.

Wilma watched her hand being moved over Scooter's head as if she were watching someone else's hand. Tentatively at first, then with more and more conviction, she began to pet him herself, and as she did her face relaxed from blank bewilderment into a great big grin.

Her eyes met mine, smiling still. Then she looked back down at Scooter and leaned forward toward him, ever so slowly. As if it was taking every ounce of strength she had, she inched her head closer and closer to the top of Scooter's head. After an agonizingly long effort, her lips rested on his fur, and she gave him the longest, loudest smooch I have ever heard.

Linda and I burst out laughing. Wilma slowly raised her head until her eyes met mine again, and the twinkle in them told me she was laughing, too.

Lorraine

Most of the places we visited had elevators. Scooter figured them out early on. He knew when that door opened to walk in, and when it opened again to walk out. He would stand facing the elevator door and get on or off as soon as it opened. I had to apologize for his lack of manners if anyone else was with us. He always went first, even if there were ladies present.

One day we took the elevator to the third floor of Platinum Ridge Nursing Center. A woman was sitting in a wheelchair near the elevator when we exited. Her hair was steely grey, straight, and cut short. She was tall with a stocky build. She was hunched forward, not moving, staring at the ground.

I said, " Hello", loud enough to get her attention. She slowly raised her head. When her eyes met mine, I asked her if she liked cats. Her expression changed from blank to puzzled. Then she spotted Scooter. She gave me a look of almost shock, and she began to chant, "Oh my God, oh my God," over and over.

Slowly she reached out both her arms to Scooter. I leaned down and stood his front feet on her lap while I hung on to the rear half of the cart, like I did with everybody in a wheelchair. But Lorraine kept coming, relentlessly, until she had taken Scooter, cart and all, into her arms. Still in slow motion, she hugged him tight against her chest. Her expression was now one of joyful disbelief that she had this treasure in her possession. She kept repeating, now to Scooter, "Oh my God, oh my God."

Lorraine haltingly lifted her head until her eyes met mine again. When they did, she gave me the fiercest, meanest look I had ever seen. She clutched Scooter even tighter to her bosom, her glare warning me in no uncertain terms that she was not letting go anytime soon, if ever.

"Uh-oh!" I thought to myself. "What do I do now? I'm going to have to fight an old lady to get my cat back!"

That was not the first time I found myself stuck in a situation with no apparent solution. A woman came storming into my clinic one day, trailed by two small children who were red-faced from crying. The woman herself looked to be on the verge of tears. She told me that her son, the bigger of the two kids, had been playing with his new pet gerbil on the living room couch. The gerbil, as rodents naturally like to do, ducked under one of the seat cushions. The kid's natural response was to grab the gerbil's tail and pull him back out. Unfortunately the kid wound up with nothing but the skin from the gerbil's tail in his hand instead of the whole gerbil. He had managed to deglove that creature's entire tail, leaving only bones and flesh still attached.

The woman then shoved a large mug, like the kind you would drink soup from, at me. Inside the mug was a bunch of shredded newspaper. The gerbil, which was actually a baby gerbil, was so small I had to root through the paper shreds with my finger to find it. When I did, I saw that other than having a skinless tail it was perfectly fine and not one bit bothered by all the drama surrounding it.

I told this Mom we would have to amputate the tail, but that was not a hard thing to do. She was so relieved I think she would have agreed to anything I suggested at that point.

I took the gerbil, mug and all, into our treatment room in back. I applied a topical anesthetic to the base of the tail. Once I was sure it was numb, I used a tiny pair of scissors designed for operating on eyes to snip off the skinless part of the tail. The tail was so tiny, not much bigger than a thread, that it didn't even bleed.

I then had to figure out how to close the skin over the remaining stump. It was way too tiny for even the smallest suture material I had, so no way could I stitch it closed. I decided to use tissue glue. During the Vietnam war, medics discovered that Super Glue worked really well for closing skin wounds. Since then it has been made in a sterile form for just that purpose and used by veterinarians everywhere.

I put a small drop of the tissue glue on the tail stump and using my thumb and forefinger I pressed the skin closed and held it for a second to let the glue set.

Apparently I was absent the day they taught us how to use glue in kindergarten. Because I now discovered that my thumb and forefinger were glued to that gerbil's tail. Thumb, tail stump, and finger were all one. It was one of those "Now what do I do?" moments, just like when Lorraine took Scooter.

I did eventually extract my flesh from that of the gerbil. I may have left some skin cells attached to its stump, but we were both separate creatures again.

Back outside the elevator at Platinum Ridge I spent a good ten minutes just standing there, feeling helpless, as Lorraine continued cooing over her prize. I decided to try diplomacy.

"Lorraine," I said to her, "Scooter and I are going to visit some of the other patients here for a while, but then we'll come right back and see you again. Okay?"

I waited, holding my breath. Lorraine slowly raised her head to meet my eyes.

"Okay," she said, drawing out the word. As I heaved a sigh of relief, she relinquished her grip on Scooter, allowing me to take him back.

Every visit after that, Lorraine was the first one we would go to see on the third floor, and we always stopped to see her again before we left. For several years I would tell whoever else was nearby the story of how I thought Lorraine had stolen my cat from me. She would laugh, a mischievous twinkle in her eye, as I laughed along with her.

One day when we stopped to see her, she didn't even look at Scooter. She had no interest in petting him, no "Oh my God." She was like that for the next few visits.

Then she was gone.

Maria

"Ciao, Bella!" I would exclaim every time I saw Maria. Maria was an elderly Italian lady with short salt-and-pepper hair and a bit of a moustache. She spoke almost no English, and those two words were all the Italian I knew. But she lit up like a Christmas tree when she saw Scooter, so the language barrier was not a problem.

Sometimes she would ask, "What he eat?"

I would say, "Spaghetti!"

"Spaghetti?!?" she'd cry. Then we'd both laugh.

One day I found Maria in her wheelchair out in the hallway. She lived in one of the not very nice nursing homes. They were chronically understaffed, and what staff they did have were overburdened. Maria was in obvious distress. She was crying and reached her arms up to me saying, "Help me! Help me!"

I looked around, but as usual no one was there. I asked her what was wrong, but she either didn't understand me or couldn't tell me. She just kept crying and reaching out, repeating, "Help me!"

I felt as helpless as she seemed. I was not trained in the care of people and I was explicitly forbidden to do anything other than visit with a patient. I was not even allowed to push a patient's wheelchair. But I very much wanted to do something for Maria.

I then had an inspired thought. I took Scooter out of his wheelcart and put him in her lap. You would have thought he was a magic wand. As soon as she wrapped her arms around him, her face lit up in a smile, the tears stopped, and all was right with the world again.

I never did find out what was wrong with Maria that day. I did figure out how to fix it, though.

Frank

Frank was a new patient at Harmarville. An older man, he was wearing a hospital gown and seated in a wheelchair with a padded foam support under his left arm. At first glance he seemed oblivious. Bob, the physical therapy tech sitting with him, called us over. Bob was one of Scooter's biggest fans and would eagerly introduce Scooter to any patient he was with.

Karen Hinkes was with us that day. "Do you like cats?" she asked Frank. Slowly he lifted his head and turned toward us. His eyes focused from a hazy empty stare to looking right at me. I smiled and put Scooter into his line of sight.

Karen was moving around Frank's wheelchair so she could lift his right arm and help him pet Scooter. But no need. Once Frank's eyes focused on the cat, he smiled and, nimble as could be, reached out and started to pet Scooter's head, scratch behind his ears, and scratch the back of his neck. Scooter was leaning into Frank, closing his eyes, and clearly loving it. While Frank and Scooter were enjoying each other's company, Karen, Bob, and I took turns talking to Frank. There was no verbal response, but his face was relaxed and happy.

After a while, Frank stopped his petting. Scooter, as he often did, turned and stared Frank right in the face.

"That look," I told him, "means, 'Hey! Who said you could stop petting me?'"

Say no more. Frank went right back to petting again. Still no words, but as we went to leave, I lifted Scooter down to the floor and turned back to see Frank smiling down at Scooter and waving good-bye.

Mass

At one nursing home our scheduled visiting day coincided with the local priest's day to come to their recreation room and deliver Mass. The residents played bingo in that room right before Mass. (First things first, right?) Scooter and I usually got there during bingo, and I tried to visit with everybody in the room before the priest got there. But sometimes we were still making the rounds when Father arrived.

Father never told me his name. He would stand at the front of the room with a forced smile on his face, silently but not very patiently waiting for me and Scooter to leave. Often, he would start Mass while we were still saying our good-byes to the people there. He was not one bit subtle about wanting Scooter and me gone. He seemed like a sour type of priest to me.

One day, just to try and lighten him up a bit, I told him on our way out that we weren't staying for Mass because I didn't think Scooter was Catholic. Stone-faced, Father was clearly not amused.

Later that same day Scooter and I were walking down the hallway outside the recreation room just as Mass was letting out. Three lovely older ladies surrounded us, taking advantage of a second chance to pet Scooter. I told them what I had said to the priest about Scooter's religion, or lack thereof.

"Oh yes, he IS Catholic!" the one lady exclaimed. "It's the one true religion, so of course he is!" I sensed her tongue was firmly planted in her cheek as she said that.

"Oh, do you think?" I asked. "Well, I don't know for sure, but I think he is a Buddhist."

"Oh no," she said as she continued to rub Scooter's head and ears. "Buddhists don't like to be scritched."

Never learned that in comparative religions class.

The Second Coming

WE VISITED MARY ONCE A MONTH FOR YEARS, AND I never saw her out of bed. She was always lying flat on her back with the covers up to her armpits. Her head and the outline of her body both looked a little flattened, as if she had been lying like that for so long gravity had taken its toll on her. Whatever her physical ailments were, her mind was perfectly fine. She would ask me each visit when I was coming back next, and she remembered. As we would come into her room, she would say, "I was expecting you, today is the twenty-second." If for some reason I was unable to come on my regular day, I would make sure to call and have someone tell Mary we weren't going to be there. Otherwise she worried, and I heard about it on our next visit.

One day Mary had some interesting news.

"Jesus came to see me last night," she said, matter-of-factly. Like she was telling me it had snowed, or they served ham barbeques for dinner.

Jesus came to visit her, I said to myself. How do I respond to that? As I have said before, I'm not very religious, so to say I was dubious would be an understatement. But I decided to play along.

"He did?' I exclaimed. "Where did He come in?"

"He came down out of the ceiling," she said, "right over there, and stood at the foot of my bed. He was really mad at me because I've been praying to the Virgin Mary. He said I should be praying to Him, not her!"

Now I was intrigued. "What did He look like?" I asked.

"Oh, He's very good-looking!" she replied.

"And what was He wearing?" I wanted to know.

"He was wearing shorts and a nice shirt," she said. "And after I said I was sorry and that I would do all my praying to Him from now on, He went back up through the ceiling and was gone."

I should have asked her if He liked cats.

Full Moon

A NURSING HOME HOUSING THREE OF OUR HOSPICE patients was fronted by a wonderfully warm receptionist named Betty. Betty fell completely in love with Scooter on our first visit there. On our next visit she was waiting for me with a list she had prepared of all the other patients in the building, besides our three hospice patients, she thought would love to see him. There must have been forty or fifty names and room numbers on that list. Since she, too, was one of those people who was very hard to say no to, our visits there became a marathon, more like our nursing home visits than our individual hospice patient visits.

The third floor of this building was for the memory-care patients. To get the elevator doors to open at that floor, you had to know the secret code. It was a four-digit number, the current day and month; for example, if it was July sixteenth, the code was 1607. Our visits to this floor could be quite entertaining. Almost all of these patients were out of their rooms, wandering about or parked in wheelchairs by the nurses' station. Some of them were pretty out of it, but most of them were engaged in lively conversations with each other or with the staff. Quite a few folks would be shouting out their opinions on whatever happened to be going on, to whoever was listening. I especially got a kick out of two ladies who would happily sing loud, raucous duets on a prompt from a nurse or aide.

One woman followed us wherever we went, but each time I tried to engage her in conversation or even smile at her, she would turn her face to the wall or duck behind a linen cart and freeze. Her rationale seemed to be: If I don't move, you can't see me. Another very elderly woman would stop me at least four or five times while we were there and ask me which way it was to the 37D bus. Her mother was waiting for her at home, you see, so she had to catch that bus.

Some of these patients were a lot cagier than they looked. They would wait by the elevator and when the doors opened, they would nonchalantly try to walk or wheel themselves into it, knowing full well they were not allowed to do that. I sometimes had to do some fast talking to distract them until the elevator doors closed safely behind me.

Most of the action on that floor took place in a big recreation room. A long table was in the center of the room, and all the patients that could fit were parked around it while one of the staff led them in some activity or other. Which, no matter how simple the game, was hard to do with all those deteriorating brains each going its own way. The staff member leading the activities was usually delighted, I think even relieved, to see Scooter and me arrive. I'd apologize for interrupting but was enthusiastically assured they would be very glad to stop and have us visit with everyone. I'd put Scooter on top of that table and he would wheel himself from one end to the other and back, stopping for pets at each little face along the way.

On one particular day I knew that the moon was going to be full that night. We got to the recreation room and found, instead of the usual calm, a chaotic scene. One woman was quite animated, walking aggressively around the room. She stomped up to two elderly men who were just standing together next to the table and screamed, "Fuck you, assholes! You're both a piece of shit!"

I didn't need the staff person, who was not so discreetly signaling me to be careful, to tell me that things were going to be a little different that day. The staffer made her way over to me and advised me to keep my body between Scooter and that woman at all times so she wouldn't see him. We watched then as the crazed lady stormed over to the windowsill and picked up a vase. It looked like it was made out of cut glass but was actually plastic, thank God, as she proceeded to smash it repeatedly into the sill. She turned, and even though we were at the other end of the room, she spotted Scooter and started to scream, "Get that filthy animal out of my room! This is MY room, and I don't want any filthy animals in here!"

She didn't have to ask twice. We beat a hasty retreat.

The next week when we visited, that same woman was calmly seated in a wheelchair pulled up to the table. She was smiling at anyone and everyone. It was such a difference I wasn't sure if she was the same person. When I mouthed, behind her back to the staff person attending, "Is this the same lady as.....?" she nodded yes.

"What a difference a day can make," I said to the staffer.

"You have no idea," she replied.

Not Everybody Likes Cats

For all the thousands of times I asked, "Would you like to pet the cat?" almost always the answer was a verbal or nonverbal, "Yes!" Almost.

I remember an old man in a wheelchair who was staring down at the ground looking so sad. "Do you like cats?" I asked. Slowly he looked up, and his eyes focused on Scooter. His face then lit up in a great big smile and he reached out his arms to him as he said, "Hello, Baby!"

I do remember one guy who glowered up at me when I asked if he wanted to pet the cat and growled, "What for?" Can't say I had an answer for that.

In the hallway outside physical therapy at Harmarville one day I saw a man in a wheelchair parked against the wall. He was in his mid-fifties, a big burly man with a shaved head and lots of tattoos. "Mr. Tough" I called him in my head. He wanted to see Scooter, so we went over and I put Scooter's front paws on the arm of his wheelchair. Mr. Tough started to pet him and asked a lot of the usual questions – how did he get hurt, how old is he, etc. As he was talking, I noticed his voice started to sound different, like it was cracking. I looked over at his face. It seemed composed. But as I watched, a tear rolled out of his left eye and down his cheek. I never let on I saw it.

I loved guys like that. They work hard to make themselves look tough and mean but they're really just big pussycats.

Another guy at Harmarville, however, was the exception that proves the rule. As soon as we approached, he started laughing and saying how cats were good for only one thing, and that was target practice.

I bit my tongue.

He went on to say how he and his buddy liked to set cats on fire, and to swing them by their tails to see how far they could throw them.

That did it. I was well aware of the need to be professional when dealing with people, both in my job and when volunteering. Stay pleasant, don't argue, if they go low, you go high, as Michelle Obama said. But this guy really got to me. Professionalism went right out the window.

I leaned close to him and with a smile on my face I said, loud enough for only him to hear, "You know, people who don't like cats were probably RATS in a previous life." Still smiling, I walked away, looking back over my shoulder once to see the dumbfounded expression on that asshole's face.

I did not feel one bit bad about saying that. Still don't.

I suppose, if I put my anger aside, I should realize that jerk was just one example of the wildly different values people can put on the same thing. I saw that all the time in my work. For example, many people scream and get on the phone to the exterminator whenever they see a rodent. I had clients who kept mice and rats as pets and loved them dearly. You would not believe how much money they spent and the lengths they went to care for those creatures. Same thing goes for snakes. My rodent and reptile owning clients were some of the most dedicated clients I had.

There was a couple who came to see me on occasion with one of their beagles. I say on occasion because I never saw them for routine exams or vaccinations. They only showed up when they had an emergency. And they never had any money, at least not that they wanted to spend, so they always argued with me about the cost of whatever care their dogs needed and tried to get me to do the cheapest treatment possible. I called them Ma and Pa Kettle in my head, as their dress and their way of talking reminded me of those old movie characters.

One day Ma and Pa arrived carrying one of their beagles whose right front paw was wrapped in a bloody rag. When I unraveled their makeshift bandage, I saw a nasty laceration that went clear through two pads and most of the flesh of the paw from one side to the other. No way this was going to be a cheap fix. I told them that wound would never heal with just a bandage, this was going to require surgery. Surgery meant anesthesia, plus antibiotics and pain medications and whatever else. I gave them an estimate for the whole procedure, then quietly cringed, waiting for the inevitable argument about money.

Instead, Pa Kettle shocked me by agreeing to the surgery and all its costs without any debate. Ma Kettle was apparently as shocked as I felt, judging by the look on her face. She turned to her husband and griped, "You wouldn't pay that much money to have MY foot fixed if I cut it!" To which Pa calmly replied, "When's the last time you brought me a rabbit?"

With that, Ma closed her mouth, opened her pocketbook, and handed over the cash.

The Moral of the Story

Scooter and I walked into a large patient room in one of our nursing homes. There were four beds in that room, but only one patient was home. She was a petite African American lady, nicely dressed in a skirt and blouse with ankle socks and sensible shoes. She was busying herself all around her part of the room, straightening and rearranging this and that. She never stopped moving. As we approached her and I said hello, she looked up and gave me a bright smile, then started to talk. And talk. And talk some more.

She was telling me a story. It was a very long story. So long that I honestly don't even remember what it was about. I just remember worrying that I was going to be stuck in that room listening to her for hours if I didn't soon figure out how to make a graceful exit. After all, we still had a lot more patients to see that day and only so much time.

Finally, thankfully, she ended her story, then gave me a satisfied look, clapped her hands together, and declared, "So you see, if the Lord lets you live, you'll learn!"

Millie's Diagnosis

I HAD THE MOST AMAZING EXPERIENCE ON ONE NURSING home visit. I walked into the physical therapy room at Platinum Ridge nursing home with Scooter and was directed to go over to an elderly woman seated in a wheelchair with a PT tech standing next to her.

"She's blind," the tech told me, although I already knew that from looking at her clouded eyes. I said hello and introduced myself, described my cat for her and told her why we were there. Her name was Millie, and she said she liked cats a lot.

I stood Scooter's front feet on her lap with her permission. She reached out with her hands and ran them over his head and down his body, feeling him more than petting him. As soon as her fingers got to the middle of his spine, she stopped.

"What happened to him?" she asked. "His back is broken." Her fingers were on the precise spot of his spinal cord injury. I was stunned, as were the two PT techs within earshot. The techs both came over and ran their hands over Scooter's back, but neither of them could feel anything different at that spot. Nor could I.

"How did you know that, Millie?" they asked. "How could you tell?"

Millie said nothing.

Had I still been in practice, I would have hired her on the spot.

I had a client once, a middle-aged woman, who owned a really nasty cat. This cat was not only terrible for us at the clinic, but it was not very nice to its owner either. All of a sudden, she told me, the cat started to jump up next to her every time she sat down and would then take its one front paw and stroke it across the owner's abdomen, from left to right, at the level of her lower rib cage. Around this time the owner turned fifty years old and, following her doctor's advice, went for her first routine colonoscopy. Guess what. She had colon cancer. Right where her cat had been stroking her. After surgery and chemo, once she was cancer-free, the cat stopped its stroking behavior and went back to being its old crabby self.

Somehow the cat knew. Just like Millie knew.

Veronica

Veronica, I was told, was going to be ninety-three years old on the following Tuesday. A petite woman with short grey hair, she was missing most of the fingers on her right hand, as well as the tips of several fingers on her left hand. She was in bed, wearing a hospital gown, but her eyes were bright as a bird's, and she had no hearing loss.

This was her first time meeting Scooter. I put him up on the bed next to her - one of his favorite places to be - and she started to pet him. She smiled, softly sweet-talking him and petting him. Suddenly she stopped. Her face clouded over, she scowled at Scooter and commanded, "Stop winking at me!"

Cats can wink?

Girls Night Out

Room 207 was a large four-bed room, with two beds on one side and two on the other. The heads of the beds were against the walls, so as a patient lay in bed, she was facing the patient in the bed across the room.

That day there were only three patients in 207. The two women on the right side of the room were sound asleep, on their backs, mouths open, softly snoring. The lady on the left side of the room was awake and sitting up, so we started to chat.

"Your roommates are asleep," I noted.

She stopped petting Scooter when I said that and shot a dirty look across the room. "That's because they were drinking all night!" she growled, pantomiming holding a cup up to her mouth and downing it in one gulp.

"Drinking?" I asked. This was, after all, a nursing home, and in five years of visiting there I had never seen anything stronger than coffee or Ensure being consumed.

"Yeah," she said. "That one," jerking her chin at the woman farthest from her, "kept asking me today, 'Why did you let me drink so much?' And I said, 'I didn't let you do anything! You did this all by yourself.'

"See that face?" She again jerked her chin in the sleeping woman's direction. "That's the face of an alcoholic!" she pronounced. And with that, the subject was closed.

All-night benders in the nursing home. I wonder what else goes on in there that we don't know about?

Birds of a Feather

TOM WAS A FRIEND OF MINE, AND A TECHNICIAN AT THE hospital where I worked. He was a big fan of Scooter. Tom's mom, Jean, had recently been admitted to a nursing home, not one of our usual ones. Tom asked if I would bring Scooter to visit her there, and I was happy to do so. While we were talking to Jean, one of her fellow patients, a woman named Monica, was wheeled in. Monica and Jean had become friends and spent a lot of time together. Tom had a big mouth and had been bragging to Monica about Scooter, so she wanted to see this famous cat for herself.

Monica was only fifty- nine years old but she had had a stroke, so her speech was hard to understand. Not impossible, but hard. One thing I learned early on in my dealings with human patients was to never pretend you understand what they're saying if you really don't. They could always tell if you were faking, and it made them mad.

Fortunately I usually had a good ear for garbled words. One late night in vet school while doing treatments in the horse barns I ran into the head equine surgeon as he was making his rounds. He had his two-year-old son with him, who was very chatty. We had a long conversation, this little boy and I. When we finished, I looked up to see the good doctor looking at me with a puzzled expression on his face.

"Could you understand him?" he asked me.

"Yes," I replied. "Why do you ask?"

"Because I can't understand a word he says!" he declared. And that was his own kid!

While Monica and Jean were petting Scooter on Jean's bed, a young male nurse named Carlos came in. Carlos had also heard Tom's bragging and wanted to see this famous cat, too. Carlos was very taken with Scooter, almost in awe. Scooter, in return, seemed quite smitten by Carlos. Scooter wheeled himself to the foot of Jean's bed and stood there facing Carlos, as close as he could get, and just stared at him.

I remarked to Tom how much Scooter seemed to be attracted to Carlos, when Monica said something I couldn't understand. Another nurse standing next to Carlos kind of winced, and asked Carlos, "Did you hear what she said?"

"I heard her," he dryly replied.

Monica spoke again, and again I couldn't understand her.

"I heard her again," grumbled Carlos.

"What did she say?" I asked.

"She said it's because I'm black like him!" We all laughed. Especially Monica.

Kiss Him Head

AFTER VISITING ALL THE PATIENTS AT HARMARVILLE Rehabilitation Hospital, now named Encompass Health Rehabilitation Hospital of Harmarville, we always stopped by one of the offices upstairs. Sally Monteleone worked there, and there has never been a greater cat lover on this earth. She always had a treat for Scooter, and a toy, every week. Often the toy was just the toe of an old sock which she had stuffed with catnip and tied shut. But those were his very favorite toys.

Sally would end our visits by telling me to, "Kiss him head!" She said it was an expression she started using when one of her cats would walk up to her and bow his head in front of her so she could kiss it. One day, she told me, her brother was visiting her, and this same cat walked up to him and bowed its head in front of him.

"What is he doing?" he asked Sally.

"He wants you to kiss him head!" she replied.

"I'm not kissing no cat on the head!" he groused. With that, the cat turned around and stood with his rear end facing Sally's brother.

"And I'm not kissing that part, either!" he exclaimed.

That seems like a good place to "end" the stories.

Suddenly It Stopped

THERE WERE HINTS, EARLY ON, BEFORE.

In 2019, Scooter turned twelve years old. Although he showed no signs of slowing down - in fact we were the busiest we had ever been - I still gave some thought to retiring him at some point. Maybe when he was fourteen. Maybe sooner. Maybe later.

The decision, apparently, was not mine to make.

In March of 2020 I was having lunch with my niece Beth and her mom, my older sister Karen. Beth was visiting from her home in Washington D.C. We got talking about all the rumors going around about this new disease called Covid. No one really knew then what we were in for, although everyone was speculating.

I told Beth I was scheduled to attend a continuing education conference later that spring in Virginia Beach at their convention center, and from what I was hearing I was getting a little nervous about being confined in a closed building with a lot of other people from all over the states. I couldn't not go, however, because I had to have the hours of CE in order to keep my veterinary license.

Beth stated flat out that my conference would be cancelled. I was shocked, really. I had never even considered that as a possibility. She told me a professional contact of hers, who worked for FEMA and was thus privy to information not yet generally available to the public, had told her that this Covid was going to be bad. Really bad. To expect a lot of things to be shut down or cancelled. That life was going to change.

I heard what she said. I can't say I believed it. Who would have, back then?

A little later in the spring of 2020, that God awful year, I was at a nursing home with my husband Steve, instead of with Scooter. We were visiting his father, Chuck. Chuck had been diagnosed with dementia in 2016. Steve moved him up from Florida that year to a graduated-care facility called Concordia close to our home. His disease had progressed, as expected, and he had been transferred to the skilled nursing unit of that facility. Scooter and I had been visiting that unit and another unit at Concordia ever since Chuck first arrived, so I was quite familiar with it. That day there was a new sign on the front door. It warned all visitors to go straight to their loved-one's room and visit only that one person. Do not go from room to room, it said.

Uh, oh. That was exactly what Scooter and I did. We would go from room to room, visiting anyone and everyone who wanted us to come in.

The very next day, one of my good friends who worked with a therapy dog called to tell me that TDI (Therapy Dogs International, the foremost group in pet therapy in the world) had sent out a notice to all its members. All pet therapy visits were to be discontinued immediately, until further notice.

I took my cue from TDI and called all the nursing homes, and the hospice, and Harmarville Rehabilitation Hospital, and told them I didn't think we should visit anymore. With that, our pet therapy work came to a screeching halt. It wasn't long before all visitors, human and animal, were banned from nursing homes and hospitals everywhere.

Life got slower and quieter. As it did for the whole world, mostly. I found myself really missing our visits, really missing the patients, and mostly really missing how good I felt inside after each visit. I think Scooter missed it, too. He no longer had scores of people to pet and adore him. Now he had only me.

I found myself filling some of the empty time thinking back on my career. It seemed like my brain was telling me old funny stories to keep me entertained and sane. I remembered Sundance, a yellow lab who suffered from severe skin allergies back in the day when cortisone was all we really had to treat the awful itching that came with them. Cortisone worked great on the itching, but had a lot of serious and potentially life-threatening side effects, so we had to use it sparingly. As a result, Sundance was itchy more often than not. He would chew and scratch, causing his owners to yell at him to stop. Which he did, but not for long, then the itching and the yelling would start all over again. His owner made me laugh one day by telling me that Sundance eventually figured out how to go into their bathroom and use his nose to close the door behind him, so he could chew and scratch to his heart's content, in peace.

I thought back on Rum Raisin, a dog I met in California. She was a medium size mutt, and the sweetest dog ever – unless you tried to pick her up. I made that mistake on our first office call. She was wagging her tail, acting as friendly as could be while I greeted her and petted her. But when I reached down to lift her up onto the exam table, she snapped at me and had I not been quick to react would have given me a nasty bite. Her owners were very apologetic, and explained that Rum had been in an earthquake a few years back, and since then did not like her feet to leave the ground. Not being a native Californian (and never experiencing an earthquake during the two years I lived there), this was something I had never considered. I did her entire exam, shots and all, sitting on the floor next to her, and she was as good as gold for all of it.

One of my favorite stories was the British client I had who owned a female bichon frise. Bichons, if you don't know them, are little white dogs that look a lot like poodles, except for a longer tail. But don't call them poodles in front of their owners! I made that mistake once and got soundly reprimanded for it. Anyway, this prim and proper lady very much wanted to breed her little bichon. Despite several tries with male dogs belonging to members of her bichon club, she was having no success. She came to see me because I was one of just a few veterinarians in Pittsburgh doing artificial insemination at that time, something I learned during my internship in California. First we did a lot of laboratory tests to make sure she was timing her breeding attempts correctly, and other tests on the males to make sure they weren't shooting blanks, if you know what I mean. When no puppies were forthcoming after several more natural breeding attempts, we went ahead with the artificial insemination. All of this took a lot of time and effort and was not cheap. But Hallelulia! She finally got pregnant. When I told her owner the good news she hugged and kissed her little bichon as she delightedly declared to her, "Oh you clever, clever girl!" Although I don't think her intelligence had much of anything to do with it.

As fate would have it (or maybe it was karma, since I was responsible, so I thought at the time, for her getting pregnant), when it came time to deliver the pups, she was unable to do so on her own, and needed a C-section. On my night on call. Late one Saturday I found myself at the hospital with the technician also on call, doing surgery on this little white dog. Surgery always made me nervous, so I was intently concentrating on what I was doing when my technician said, "Uh, Dr. Kennon?"

"What?" I snapped, keeping my head down and my eyes on my patient instead of looking up at him. I had been removing the puppies, one at a time, from the uterus I had cut open, and handing them, still in their amnionic sacs, to my tech. It was his job to open the sac and rub the puppies with a towel to dry them off and get them breathing on their own.

"Uh, Dr. Kennon?"

"What, Dana?" I snapped again, still not looking up at him.

"I didn't know bichons came in black," he replied.

They don't. Once surgery was finished, I went to talk to the owner anxiously waiting in the lobby. When I told her that she was the proud owner of four very expensive black mutts, she swore, in her gentile British accent, "That son of a bitch! I'm going to kill him!" Turns out there was a small black mixed breed dog that lived next door to her, who had been, of course, very interested in her little bichon each time she went into heat. Apparently, he had somehow figured out how, THROUGH THE FENCE, to mate with that female, who no doubt was being more than cooperative, since her hormones were telling her that was the absolute right thing to be doing at that moment.

I had another client from one of the city neighborhoods come to see me with her handsome male doberman. She told me her big dobie had climbed the fence between her yard and her neighbor's when her neighbor's dog was in heat and did the dirty deed with her over there. Her neighbor, on seeing this, came screaming over to my client's house threatening to have her dog arrested for rape. To which my client calmly replied, "Oh, no, that was no rape. She CALLED him down!" She was right.

I chuckled remembering all the times I performed a sex change in the exam room. By this I mean the new owners of a darling puppy or kitten would come in thinking it was one sex, when on examination I found it to be the opposite sex. Surprisingly, kids always got really mad at me when I gave them the news and refused to believe it. They were adamant that I was wrong. I learned it was best to just give up trying to convince them and leave it to Mom and Dad to take it from there. One really macho guy, a truck driver, came in with his new doberman puppy he had named Spike. When Spike turned out to be a girl, he was flabbergasted. All he could say was, "Now what do we call him?"

I always volunteered to be on call Christmas day. I had no kids, so the day didn't mean that much to me. The other doctors who did have kids were very appreciative. One Christmas day a woman came in with her dog who had been acting very strangely. She said it was stumbling and weaving around the house and had been dribbling urine. A quick exam told me the dog was stoned. Dogs love to eat marijuana, and this one had obviously done so. I was puzzled, though, because that woman did not look at all like the marijuana-smoking type. When I told her my diagnosis and reassured her the dog would be fine once he slept it off, her face clouded up and she grabbed her cell phone out of her purse, looking like she was ready to murder someone. Turns out her kid was home from college for the holiday, and Mom figured out pretty quick where the dope came from. "I asked him if he had any of that stuff, and he swore to me he didn't!" she growled. I'm thinking that kid's Merry Christmas was not so merry.

I remembered learning a good lesson about not judging a book by its cover when I was in California. I worked for a year at a large practice in Walnut Creek, a bedroom community to San Francisco. Our clientele were mostly well-to-do. My first appointment one day was a woman who looked to be anything but. She was dressed like a bag lady in shabby old clothes. She was wearing sneakers that were more hole than shoe, with mismatched socks, and her hair was a tangled mess. She had a cat with her, in a beat up old carrier, that had a nasty abscess. That practice was quite regimented when it came to what we were required to charge for various procedures. The price for treating an abscess, lancing and draining it plus antibiotics and pain medications, was pretty much set in stone. I would have liked to cut some corners for this woman, as it looked like she did not have two nickels to rub together, but my hands were tied. I told her what we needed to do to make her cat better, and how much it would cost, and she quietly gave me the okay to proceed.

Later that day she came to pick up her cat. As she left the exam room, after I had given her all the aftercare instructions, she went out to the front desk to pay, and I snuck out to the lobby. I was curious to see how she had gotten to our hospital. Public transportation was not readily available in that area, other than taxis which were expensive. To my profound surprise I watched as a fancy limousine drove up to our door when she stepped outside. The driver, dressed in an immaculate chauffeur's uniform, got out of the car and quickly stepped over to the passenger door, which he held open as my "bag lady" client got in. Off they went, as a nagging voice in my head said, "That will teach you. Never assume."

I seemed to have had a lot of great dane patients when I was practicing. I wonder if the owners got a kick out of seeing my little five-foot self handling their giant dogs. Nice dogs, most of them, but not the brightest bulbs in the chandelier. I got a call early one morning from our local police, saying they were at a neighbor's house whose dog had managed to get a large fishhook stuck to his lip, and then proceeded to get his front paw stuck to the same hook while trying to paw it off his lip. The cops brought him in to the clinic walking on his three unhooked legs, but otherwise just as happy and unconcerned as if nothing was wrong. When his owners came to pick him up later that day, minus the fishhook, I said to them, "Here's your catch of the day!" I don't think they appreciated my humor.

Another dane came to see me on Good Friday one year with, I kid you not, a large nail protruding from the middle of his paw. This dog, too, was acting like this was a completely normal thing, having a five-inch nail sticking up out of his foot. No brain, no pain I liked to say. I was a little spooked by the symbolism – a nail in the middle of his paw, on Good Friday? Not exactly the Second Coming, but still....

The craziest great dane I ever saw came in to the exam room one day and immediately jumped up onto the exam table, landing perfectly on all four feet. I had been in practice for a lot of years by then and had impatiently stood by hundreds of times while an owner would try to get his or her pet to jump up on the exam table by itself, without being lifted.

They never did. Never. Until this dane. But as soon as he landed on the table, he jumped back down to the floor, then back up on the table, then down to the floor, and on and on it went. He was there for me to draw blood for a heartworm test. I stood there watching this spectacle, and I thought to myself, "How am I going to get this dog to hold still long enough for me to get a blood sample from him?" He was way too big and strong for me to physically restrain him. Then from out of nowhere I had an inspired thought. I took a cotton ball, a simple cotton ball, and showed it to the dog. Then I slowly placed said cotton ball on the seat of the chair in the room. The dog was mesmerized. He stood stock still, staring at that cotton ball for as long as it took me to hit his cephalic vein with my syringe and draw the required amount of blood. Once I picked up the cotton ball, like when the hypnotist snaps his fingers, the rodeo resumed.

My entertaining musings did bring along with them some not so pleasant memories. I remembered one day when I had to put a litter of seven puppies to sleep, along with two other unrelated dogs. All of these euthanasias were justified, and the right thing to do. But I left the clinic that day feeling like my karma had suffered some serious damage. I went straight to the local blood bank and donated blood for the first time. I felt a little better after that.

The saddest euthanasia I ever had to do was for an elderly couple. They told me they both had serious health issues and found themselves with no choice but to move to a nursing home. The nursing home, however, did not take pets. They had no family or friends that would take their elderly lhasa apso, and they could not bring themselves to take her to a shelter where she would be in the care of total strangers. So they made the best decision for her, but the absolute hardest decision for them, to have her put to sleep. I have always cried whenever I have ended a life, no matter how justified. I cried for a long time after that one.

My worst memory was of the office call that almost ended my life. It was evening office hours, and I was seeing a golden retriever for his annual exam. Back in the day, there was no such thing as a mean golden retriever. They were the nicest dogs on the planet. But like any breed that gets popular, they got overbred, and bad temperaments along with a host of medical problems started to show up in those beautiful dogs. I had been seeing this particular golden for several years. He was never especially friendly, but he had never been aggressive to me. I started my exam at his head, looking in his mouth and his ears, things that a lot of dogs do not like. No reaction. I then went behind him and squatted down to reach up and palpate his abdomen. Being behind and below a dog are actions that normally do not threaten them in any way. In addition, dogs that are about to attack will normally give a warning first, a growl or a change in their body language. This dog was not normal. Next thing I knew he reared around and was at my throat, snapping and snarling, knocking me off my feet and onto my butt on the exam room floor where I was helpless to defend myself. Thankfully the owner, who was oblivous to what was going on, still somehow managed to hold onto the dog's leash, so he didn't get to my fallen body. But he did rip my right forearm, which I had instinctively thrown up in front of my neck, wide open and also left three deep punctures in my right hand and wrist. It was off to the ER, where, as fate would have it, another client of mine was the attending doctor there that night. As she cleaned and stitched my wounds, and the shock of what had just happened sunk in, I started to sob. It wasn't from pain. It was from fear. I gave serious thought to never going back to work after that. I did go back, but it wasn't easy.

One funny thing about that awful event was that it happened right before Halloween. At my Halloween party that year, lots of people noticed my nasty arm wound and said to me, "Wow, that looks really real!"

Three years later that same dog had to be put to sleep. Another doctor at our clinic did the deed. I had refused to ever see that dog again, for obvious reasons. I asked my colleague to let me know when the dog was dead and before it was placed in the body bag. She did. I went back to the room where the dog's body was lying on a table, and I punched him square in the face. Hurt my hand, but the rest of me felt really good.

Scooter had his own ways of dealing with the quiet and the boredom, I soon found out. Steve and I had inherited a rottweiler, Bruno, 125 pounds big, a year before this. You may remember I have mentioned him before. Steve's best friend of forty years, Harry, who had been the best man at our wedding, had died suddenly and unexpectedly. Harry was a widower with no kids and no other living family. Unbeknownst to us, he had left everything to Steve, including this very large dog, who I'm pretty sure had never seen a cat before coming to live with us. Bruno wasn't mean or aggressive to Scooter, but he had absolutely no cat manners whatsoever. Scooter found him to be totally obnoxious. To avoid Bruno, Scooter took to staying upstairs, where the rottie never went, all the time. One day, not long after his forced retirement, Scooter came to the top of the steps, looked down, and yowled. A really loud yowl. I had been reading in the living room and was so startled by his cry that I jumped and flew up those stairs, thinking he was hurt or something else was very wrong. When I got there, I discovered that not only was he perfectly fine, but all he had wanted was for me to pet him. He had summoned me from all the way upstairs just for some attention. No doubt he missed his pet therapy days.

I had another volunteer activity at that time besides the pet therapy. After retiring from private practice in 2016, I started working with a nearby animal shelter. I was their primary veterinarian. Covid or no Covid, the work I did there had to go on.

Early on in my shelter experience, I found myself getting attached to a tiny black kitten in our care. Getting attached to the shelter animals is a serious occupational hazard in that business. I have yet to meet anyone who works in a shelter that doesn't have at least one pet of their own adopted from there. With four dogs at home, I had been able to resist adopting any more dogs pretty easily. However, that was the only time in my adult life I had owned only one cat.

One day I was sitting out on my deck. Scooter was sitting on the ottoman in front of me, facing me. I said to him, "Scooter, what would you think if I brought a kitten home from the shelter?"

He looked right at me, leaned over towards me, and bit me! Right on my arm! He didn't draw blood, but that bite hurt! It was pretty clear the answer was no when it came to any more cats.

In 2021, a year into Scooter's forced retirement, I was consulting with one of the shelter's foster pet parents over the phone. She was caring for a litter of three tiny orphaned kittens. One of them, the smallest one, was having gastrointestinal problems, one after another. She'd call me about one thing, I would suggest a remedy, it would get better, then something else would come up. I'll spare you the gross details. I finally asked the lady if I could take the kitten home with me for a few days so I could see for myself what was going on. She happily agreed.

The bathroom adjoining my bedroom had been a makeshift hospital room for a number of creatures over the years. If I didn't feel comfortable leaving an animal alone in the hospital overnight, or if it was a bird or other exotic pet that the staff, well-trained but only with dogs and cats, didn't really know how to handle, it came home with me. Having done that so many times before, I wasn't worried about what Scooter might think about having a kitten in there. The door to the bathroom would stay shut, and he would not have to deal with that kitten at all.

Home the little guy came. It took me only twenty-four hours to get his digestive issues resolved. That's when he morphed from quiet, I-don't-feel-good kitten to crazy, yee-haw, rock-and-roll kitten! I had not had a kitten in my house for over twenty years. When Scooter arrived, my other two cats were in their teens, and he was already almost a year old, past the crazy kitten stage. I had forgotten how nuts they were. Certifiably nuts! Everything was a toy! The baseboard! The wall! My sandal! After two days of him bouncing off the walls, literally, in that tiny bathroom, I decided to take a chance and open the door to my bedroom.

Out he rocketed. Scooter, much to my surprise, seemed fascinated by him. He showed no signs of being mad or annoyed, even when the kitten, who I was calling Crackers because he kept cracking me up, would hurl his tiny not even one-pound body at Scooter in play attack mode. Scooter watched him constantly. I never had to wonder where the kitten was. I only had to look at Scooter and follow his gaze. Remember, he had been confined to my upstairs with no patient visits or any other stimulation for a year by then. This must have been welcome entertainment.

That night I said, "Scooter, you and I will be up on the bed to sleep. That's a kitten-free zone." Not thinking tiny Crackers could get himself up onto my tall bed. Wrong! It took him all of five minutes to figure out how to climb up on the chair next to my bed, walk across the bedside table, and jump from there right onto my pillow. Even so, Scooter seemed fine with the three of us sleeping together. Except for the one time Crackers walked across my chest in the middle of the night and started to bat at Scooter's ears. Crackers got hissed at for that.

After four days of kitten craziness, I took Crackers back to the shelter. He was a brown tabby cat, as was his female littermate. They both got adopted into their forever homes that very week. The third kitten in that litter, however, was an all-black cat. Black cats, and dogs for that matter, are always the last to get adopted at shelters. No one really seems to know why. One week went by, then two weeks. That poor little kitten, who was every bit as charming and entertaining as his brother Crackers, was still there, all alone in his cage with no mom and no siblings. I couldn't stand it. I announced to the staff that if he was still there after one more week, I was taking him home.

He was, and I did.

Scooter now had a little brother. I named him CrackerJack, Jack for short. It turned out to be a good thing for everyone concerned. I would often find Jack and Scooter sleeping all curled up together. Trying to feed them different diets was a waste of time, as they would eat out of each other's bowls. They liked to groom each other, though Jack got tired pretty quickly of being groomed and would meow and try to squirm away. Scooter would grab whatever part of Jack was closest with his teeth and held him down till he quit squirming. The grooming would then resume.

Occasionally Scooter would swat Jack, usually well-deserved. But not often. It's hard, when you only have two good legs, to pick one of them up and whack someone without falling over. Jack, for his part, took advantage of Scooter's lack of feeling in his rear half to use Scooter's tail as a very fun cat toy. I'm sure he only got away with it because Scooter couldn't feel what was going on back there.

That was what Scooter's retirement looked like it was going to be, for the foreseeable future. A quiet, comfy life with a goofy but affectionate little brother, and me, for companionship.

If I have learned anything in this life, it is that the future is not foreseeable.

How It Ended

IT HAD BEEN FIFTEEN MONTHS OF FORCED RETIREMENT come June 2021 when one day the phone rang. It was Jayme White, the recreational director at Concordia, the nursing home where my father-in-law had lived. Chuck had passed away during the height of Covid. It might have been from Covid, as that facility did eventually have a small outbreak of cases. It might have been the dementia finally playing out. Either way, considering how he was at the end, it was a blessing.

Jayme was calling to say that Concordia was opening up to volunteers again and asked if Scooter and I would be willing to come back. I would have to sign in at the front desk and have my temperature taken there, but we were welcome to come. I was elated, and eagerly arranged a day and time to visit.

While talking to Jayme I suggested we maybe visit just a few people this time around, instead of the previous routine of going room to room to room. I reminded her that Scooter was older now, thirteen years old to be exact, so maybe we should take things a little easier. That conversation was a waste of breath. We got to Concordia only to receive a long list of room numbers and names of people to visit in both of the buildings we'd been going to. I sighed, and off we went.

It was glorious - like that fifteen-month hiatus had never happened. Even though the nursing home population was more stable than that of Harmarville, there were still a lot of new faces along with his old fans. Scooter was a rock star, charming old and new alike, spreading happiness and inspiration to everyone we visited. They all loved him, he seemed to love being there, and I know I was loving it.

It felt so good to be back.

That night I fell asleep, Scooter snuggled next to me on my right side as always, with a smile on my face.

The next morning I pulled back the covers to find the bottom sheet had a big wet spot where Scooter had been lying. I picked him up and saw that his diaper was completely soaked, so full of urine that it had leaked out through the slit I cut in it for his tail. That had never happened before. I hurried him into the shower stall, removed his soggy diaper, and was shocked to find that his urine was bloody. It was so bloody it looked more like blood than urine. He had had bloody urine once before, after jumping off my bed and landing awkwardly in the middle of the night. That time the blood resolved over a few days, and he seemed otherwise just fine. I figured he must have broken a blood vessel in his bladder, landing on it when it was full. This time the blood was worse. And there was more of it. Despite how much urine was in his diaper, there was still a lot of it left in his bladder. It took a while to express all of the bloody urine out of his bladder. Finally, many baby wipes later, he was clean and empty and in a fresh diaper.

I put him down, and he scooted off to the library next to my bedroom to bask in the sunlight that came through the big picture window in there, like he did most mornings.

I had to go to the shelter that morning. I was gone for maybe two or three hours. When I got back, Scooter had not moved. He was in the exact same position he had been when I left. When I reached for him, he let out a yowl, saying, "I'm in pain, don't touch me." That's when I knew something was really wrong.

I called the veterinary hospital I had been going to with my pets since I retired from practice myself. Like all veterinary facilities during Covid, they were swamped. But they knew me well. To be quite frank, most of the time when a client calls the vet and says there is something really wrong with their pet, it turns out to be not much of a big deal. When I said there was something really wrong with Scooter, they knew I was not just whistling Dixie. They told me to come right down, and they would squeeze me in as soon as they could.

I carefully settled Scooter into his carrier, seat-belted it into the passenger seat of my car, and drove like a bat out of hell. On the way there, and again multiple times while we sat for what seemed like forever in their waiting room, he let out that awful yowl. It sounded to me like the cry a blocked cat makes. Male cats sometimes form crystals in their urine, which in turn form a plug at the tip of their penis, preventing them from being able to urinate. As their bladder gets fuller and fuller, it gets really painful, and they yowl in a way that, once you have heard it a time or two, you know is coming from a blocked cat before you so much as lay a hand on him. But since he had just passed a ton of urine only a few hours before, I reasoned that explanation can't be the problem here.

After a long wait, Shelley, a technician who used to work at my old practice before coming to this one, and who was a friend, came out to the waiting room and escorted us back to the treatment area. Once there, they took an x-ray of Scooter, and sure enough his bladder was blocked.

One of the things I liked about this hospital was that they let me do my own veterinary thing whenever possible, just with their equipment and techs. Shelley and I got to work. I passed a urinary catheter into Scooter's bladder to let it empty. The urine, being so bloody, was coming out very slowly instead of the usual gush when the obstruction is removed. As his bladder emptied he was not perking up the way cats usually do. I took his temperature. It was low. He was cold to the touch, and almost stuporous.

Shelley and I placed an intravenous catheter in his front leg and started him on IV fluids. We drew a blood sample, which she took to their in-house lab to analyze, and wrapped him up in warm blankets with hot-water bottles inside them. I gave him an antibiotic injection, as bacteria love to grow in bloody urine. The doctor who owns the practice, Dr. Rapsinski, came in and did a quick ultrasound (a technology that didn't exist when I was in school, so I don't know one end of an ultrasound machine from the other) of his bladder to make sure there were no stones or tumors or anything else weird in there. I then hugged Scooter tight while I waited for the blood results.

When an animal is unable to urinate for a period of time, its kidney values and potassium levels on bloodwork will become elevated. That was the case with Scooter. I hoped that explained why he was still so depressed and hypothermic. I bundled him into his carrier and took him, as well as a supply of IV fluids, back home to my bathroom (once again a makeshift hospital room) to watch over him as the fluids and his now unobstructed urine flow hopefully got him back to normal.

That night I slept, if you can call it that, on a blanket on my bathroom floor, in front of the dog crate Scooter was in. He just laid in whatever position I put him. Now and again he would moan, and I would gently turn him onto his other side. He had no interest in food or water or anything. He just laid there. As the hours went by and he didn't improve, I got a sick feeling in my stomach. That feeling you get when, no matter how hard you wish things were otherwise, you know they aren't going to end well.

If having a blocked urinary bladder was his only problem, he should have been coming around. His temperature should have been back to normal, he should have been more active, he should have been getting better. He wasn't. That meant something else, something worse, must be going on. It was hard to think clearly, as tired and worried as I was. I forced myself to take off my mom hat and put on my doctor hat in order to logically put the pieces of this puzzle together. Only one diagnosis made any sense to me. Because of all the blood in his bladder, and how badly distended that bloody bladder had been, he must have thrown a clot to his brain. A stroke. If I was right, the chances of fixing this were dismal.

Normally I prided myself on my diagnostic abilities. This time I prayed I was wrong.

People who suffer strokes have no choice but to go on living, no matter how severely handicapped their brain damage leaves them, until they die on their own. This is one area where veterinary medicine is and always has been far ahead of human medicine. Veterinarians have the option of euthanasia for our patients. We can choose to end the suffering when life is no longer worth living. If Scooter had sustained serious brain damage, I was not going to let him suffer.

Come morning nothing had changed. He was still cold and zombie-like. I took him back to the veterinary hospital and had Shelley repeat his bloodwork. With all the IV fluids I had given him overnight, his blood values should have been back to normal. But maybe they weren't, and maybe that was why he was still doing so poorly. I was grasping at straws.

The blood results were normal.

I knew what I had to do.

I told Shelley I wanted her to give me two things. First, I wanted enough IV fluids to last another twenty-four hours. I had to give him the benefit of the doubt. Second, I wanted a syringe of euthanasia solution. She nodded and wordlessly got both things for me.

That night I slept again on a blanket on the bathroom floor, as close as I could get to Scooter without actually being in the crate with him. At first there was no change from the previous night. Then around midnight his moans started coming closer together. He became more restless. Nothing I did seemed to help him settle.

At four AM, I repositioned him yet again and I must have dropped off to sleep. I was awakened by a sound at 4:15. I jumped up and saw Scooter having a seizure. That proved to me that his brain was seriously damaged.

"No more," I said to him, grabbing his shaking body and cradling him in my arms. "No more pain. No more." I injected the contents of the euthanasia syringe into his IV catheter.

His now still body seemed so heavy. His fur felt so soft. His legs hung limp. His eyes were closed.

He was gone.

Clutching him to my chest, I rocked back and forth on the floor as I sobbed. I don't know how long I stayed there like that. When the tears finally slowed, I wrapped his body in his favorite blanket. I took down all the IV tubes and bags and disassembled the crate. I disposed of the syringes and put the thermometer and towels and everything else away. The bathroom was now just a bathroom again... only with a small blanket-wrapped package on the floor.

You don't just go back to bed after something like that. I went downstairs and did my usual morning chores, only two hours earlier than usual. The chickens weren't even off their roosts when I fed and watered them, and they gave me dirty chicken looks for waking them up so early. I had to use a flashlight to walk the dogs, it was still so dark outside. I moved through my routine in a daze. I was totally numb.

Chores done, I sat down at my laptop and wrote an email, which I sent to everyone I felt needed to know. It was his eulogy.

"At 4:30 this morning, Scooter went to heaven.

"Tuesday of this week, we visited a nursing home for the first time since Covid shut us down fifteen months ago. He was a rock star. Brought so much happiness to over 20 patients. The next morning, he suffered some sort of cerebral event-- a stroke, I suspect. We tried treatment, but no response. I held him in my arms as the injection eased him out of this world.

"He was not just a pet. He was my partner. Together we brought joy to hundreds of people, many of whom had precious little joy in their lives. He changed my life. He opened my heart. He opened my soul.

"This is not how it was supposed to end. One more thing on my list of things I want to discuss when I meet my maker. My grief is crippling. But I will remember him and all we did together, and life goes on.

"Love to all of you."

Then I did go back to bed. I was exhausted. I slept for three hours.

When I got up, I found my husband Steve and asked him to dig a grave for Scooter. He had already done so, while I was sleeping. He had heard my sobs earlier, and he knew.

Scooter is buried above my garden, amongst the graves of all my other pets from the last thirty years. There is a stone on his grave that says, simply, "Scooter. Therapy Cat."

You'll remember I mentioned that Linda Wilson Fuoco, the *Pittsburgh Post-Gazette* reporter who wrote about Scooter several times, would go on to write about him once more. A week after his death, her column "Pet Tales," which usually consisted of four or five stories about different pets, was about only one pet that day. Scooter. It was his obituary. This is some of what she wrote.

"Despite paralysis, Scooter was always moving on therapy visits.

"Therapy cats like Scooter are rare gems. Not many cats are comfortable leaving their homes to travel in cars to hospitals and nursing homes where many strangers will hold them and pet them. And none of them are like Scooter, who used a cart to get around because his hind legs were paralyzed when his back was broken as a kitten.

"So many beloved pets have died in the last year. Facebook and other social media accounts are filled with touching tributes and remembrances. Scooter merits a Pet Tales obituary because he really was one in a million.

"His front legs trotting briskly in front of two fast-spinning rear wheels, Scooter was quite a sight in the halls of Encompass Health Rehabilitation Hospital of Harmarville and other places he visited. He was a special inspiration in rehabilitation centers, visiting people who had also lost the use of their legs.

"'I'm in a wheelchair. He's in a wheelchair,' said one patient. 'If he can do it, I can do it.'

"In Dr. Kennon's eulogy she wrote, 'My grief is crippling, but I will remember him and all we did together, and life goes on.'

"At this house, life goes on with rottweiler Bruno, 6, mixed-breed dogs Lena, 12, and Razzie, 13, dachshund/yorkshire terrier mix Augustus UnderDog, 5, and an unexpected bonus cat named CrackerJack.

"And life goes on."

Before Scooter, I never did any kind of volunteer work. My life felt full enough with my career, my home life, and my hobbies. Now I can't imagine not doing volunteer work, for as long as I am able.

It will never be pet therapy again, most especially never with a cat. There will never be another Scooter. But I will always volunteer in some way. Not for the reasons you may think. Yes, it's good to give back, and yes, it's good to help your fellow man, etc., etc. Those reasons are all fine and noble.

The real reason is because volunteering is good for me. It keeps me sharp. It makes me feel good. It helps me keep things in perspective. It keeps me engaged and active.

Most of all, it's good for my soul. A whole, whole lot of God-blesses worth.

Thank you, my Doots, for that gift.

Epilogue

YEARS AGO I TOLD A FRIEND OF MINE THAT I WAS THINKING of writing a book about Scooter. I expected her to say something like, "Oh, that's nice!" Or maybe, "Good for you!" Or, "That's a great idea!" Instead, she gripped my arm with both hands, and with a horrified look on her face she screeched, "Don't make him die in the end! Don't let it be like *Marley and Me*! I couldn't stand that!"

My plan for this book was to put a "Spoiler Alert" in the foreword saying, "Don't worry, Scooter is alive and well at the time of my writing this, and enjoying a well-deserved retirement."

You know what they say about plans.

I wrote this book anyway because it was a story I felt needed to be told. As you know, I am a veterinarian, and writing courses were not on the curriculum at vet school. I am not a writer. I knew I needed help. I got it.

First and foremost I was helped by my niece Beth McNamara. I could not have written this book without her. A long time ago she told me to keep notes on my experiences with Scooter, and sent me a journal to use for that. A large part of the book came from the pages of that journal. When it came time to actually start writing, she sent me a book by Stephen King, of all people, called *On Writing. A Memoir of the Craft*. That book was extremely helpful. (Also very entertaining. I am now a Stephen King fan.) Finally she was my primary editor. I always read the acknowledgements at the end of every book I enjoy, and almost always the author gushes profuse and flowery praise about their editor. Now I know why.

My good friend Shelley Bates was my first reader. I held my breath waiting to hear what she thought. I was full of doubts, doubts that intensified the longer I waited. Days went by. No phone call or text from Shelley. Finally a large envelope from her arrived in the mail. It contained the copy of the book I had sent to her to read. I was sure she must be too afraid of hurting my feelings to tell me to my face how awful she thought the book was.

She loved it. I was so happy and relieved, I cried for an hour.

I learned many things from both of them. From Beth I learned that I use the words "and" and "but" and "so" way too much. From Shelley I learned that I use too many commas, that I should number my pages, and that "motherfucker" is all one word. Good things to know.

My reporter friend Linda Wilson Fuoco helped me, unknowingly I think, by allowing me to believe I could actually do this. In an email she said, "I can tell from your emails you know how to write." Coming from someone who writes for a living, that was momentous.

So many things came together to make this book happen, just like so many things came together to make my life with Scooter happen, that I have to believe there has been a higher power guiding the process. That always helps.

Who knows where the book will go from here? Not so long ago it was hard to think it would ever get this far. Maybe someone will make it into a movie. Wouldn't that be something!

I think Meryl Streep should play me. Good luck finding a cat to play Scooter.

*There, Sally, I wrote the damn book.
If only I could kiss him head.*